Shoestring Marketing

SHOESTRING MARKETING

Larry Mersereau

Griffin Publishing

Glendale, California

Illustrations:	CorelDraw
Book Design:	Mark M. Dodge
Copy Editor:	Freda Yoshioka
Cover Design:	Clinton Wade Graphics

10 9 8 7 6 5 4 3 2 1

ISBN 1–882180–57–7

Griffin Publishing

544 Colorado Street

Glendale, California 91204

Telephone: 1–800–423–5789

Manufactured in the United States of America

Contents

Acknowledgments

In late 1994, I attended a seminar conducted by Mark Victor Hansen, a well-known speaker and coauthor of a best-selling book. At that seminar, Mark singled me out and challenged me to finish a book that was half-baked at the time. He said to believe that I could finish it and I did. That book you now hold in your hand.

One of the things that Mark told us to do was to start a list of the people we most want to meet. He said to believe that we could meet these people and we would.

Three months later, while traveling to an international speaking engagement of my own, I was listening to one of my favorite audio casettes called "How to Build High Self Esteem" by Jack Canfield.

It occurred to me at 40,000 feet that Jack Canfield, Mark's coauthor for *Chicken Soup for the Soul*, belonged on my list of people to meet. I had listened to Jack's tape set a half-dozen times in the previous year. Through his tapes, Jack had literally changed my life.

Two weeks after that trip, an invitation arrived in the mail. It was an invitation to attend Jack Canfield's Self Esteem Facilitation Skills workshop. I had to go!

Two weeks before the seminar, at the National Speakers Association's national convention, I got to meet Jack Canfield and renew my acquintance with Mark Victor Hansen.

By then, I was in the final stages of writing the first draft of this book. When the seminar started, I still hadn't come to an agreement with a publisher and many of the chapters were incomplete. I was more than a little frustrated.

But I didn't stop believing it would happen.

One of the publishers I had been talking to was Griffin Publishing. During the week of the Canfield seminar, I spoke with Bob Howland, president of Griffin. Bob Howland's office is a few blocks from the hotel where the seminar was being held! Bob brought over a book contract and I went for it.

The energy I gained during that seminar—eight days with Jack and a visit from Mark—carried me forward to finish the first draft. Considerable rewriting of several chapters was called for. The energy remained and I finished the final draft two days before the deadline.

Jack Canfield and Mark Victor Hansen—thank you for your inspiration, your encouragement and your confidence.

This book is only the first one!

Larry Mersereau

September, 1995

Chapter 1

Planning to Succeed

You probably recognize Alice's quandary in Lewis Carroll's *Alice in Wonderland*:

> One day Alice came to a fork in the road and saw a Cheshire cat in a tree. "Which road do I take?" she asked. His response was a question: "Where do you want to go?" "I don't know," Alice answered. "Then," said the cat, "it doesn't matter."

Unfortunately, many business owners make important decisions every day with the same lack of direction because they don't have a plan. It's been said, "If you're not planning to succeed, you're planning to fail."

The purpose of this book is to bring you the basics of marketing so you can plan to succeed. It's a Marketing 101 for the business owner. Whether you have studied marketing or not, you'll find this short course invaluable.

Many small business owners have to operate all aspects of their business, from payroll, to overhead, to marketing, on a shoestring. Even on a shoestring budget, successful marketing calls for advance planning and the coordination of the five building blocks of marketing. This book will help you do this—on a shoestring.

The topic of marketing is broken down into five manageable pieces called the Five Building Blocks of Marketing. These building blocks, critical to any marketing strategy, are explained in the first portion of the book while practical methods for executing your own marketing plan comprise the rest of the book.

The Big Five

Broadly speaking, the process of marketing is the movement of goods from the producer to the consumer. Specifically, this process is based on five interdependent activities: market research, product development, pricing, distribution and promotion.

These are the five building blocks of marketing. It doesn't matter whether you are an individual working from your kitchen table or a Fortune 500 corporation; you must manage all five components of marketing.

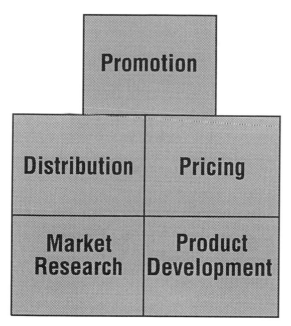

Market research sounds very technical and extremely difficult. However, the fact is, no matter how excellent your product or service, it will not make a profit if you don't identify, locate and reach your target customer. In simple terms, Chapter 2 will look at how you can find and identify the customers who are likely to do business with you.

Product development is often the first step in marketing. For example, say you have a great idea and decide to start your own business. Eventually, you may want to add to your product line. Or, perhaps yours is a business that resells products manufactured by another business. In any case, the products and variety in your line of products are your *product mix*. Chapter 3 talks about how to manage that mix for profitability.

Pricing, detailed in Chapter 4, is a balancing act between the consumer's idea of value, the competitor's price and profitability. Many small businesses go bankrupt by engaging in price competition, struggling to hold on to customers while losing money on each transaction. Advance planning will help prevent that fate.

The business owner must understand where he or she fits into the distribution system. As the product moves from producer to end user, every step adds expense, time and risk to the distribution process. Distribution must be carefully managed, as outlined in Chapter 5.

Promotion is the last of the five building blocks to be discussed because the other four will qualify or eliminate the media and methods you choose for promotion. Your promotion planning and execution will be effective if you first address market research, product development, pricing and distribution.

But first...

Statistics from the U.S. Small Business Administration show that most new businesses fail within five years of inception. Many that survive beyond the first five years continue to lose money consistently but are propped up by owners who have sufficient capital and commitment to keep the business operating.

In many of these cases, business owners are so busy putting out the fires of the day that they never find time to plan for the future. Planning must be a priority. Your business' success—in fact, its survival—depends on it.

Where do you want to go? What do you hope to accomplish in the next five years? Do you plan to provide a living for your family with the business' profits? Do you want to build a business that is rich with capital so it can withstand unprofitable periods? Are you trying to make some kind of impact on your community or the world? Maybe you want to leave a thriving business to your children.

Also consider what you want to do for your customers. This may sound obvious, but a business that is not focused on customer satisfaction will have a rough time in the coming years. The customer must be integral to your "grand plan". Customers are a part of your business. They are, in fact, the most important part! Without them, your business does not exist.

The answers to these questions will form your grand plan and will guide you in many of your planning decisions. Does your strategy call for short-term profit or long-term growth? Are profits or stability your top priorities? Your grand plan contains your answers.

To stay focused on their plans, most successful business owners have formulated a very clear, brief mission statement. The mission statement may evolve over the years but, whatever the stage of your business, it does provide focus and guidance for many of your marketing and planning decisions.

Many business owners have a difficult time writing a mission statement because they feel like it must be carved in stone. However, no part of the planning process should be that rigid.

A mission statement should simply declare:

Who your customers are;

What you do or provide for them;

Where you do it; and,

What makes you different.

The following is a sample mission statement.

Sample Mission Statement: We are the only store in the western suburbs offering top-quality kitchen products for professional chefs and serious home cooks. Our customers recognize and appreciate the difference quality cookware can make in the outcome of their favorite recipes.

This clearly states who the business' customers are: professional chefs and serious home cooks. The business provides quality cookware that is probably not available in most department stores. The business' domain is the western suburbs and its customers are very picky about their food.

This business is clearly focused on a specific type of customer, product line, and geographic area. By being this focused, every marketing decision becomes simple. Whether the business is considering an advertising medium, a new product, pricing decisions, or distribution options, its decisions will be based on its answers to the questions: "Does this fit our mission?" "Does this reach, serve and appeal to our target customer?"

The statement of differentiation, or, why the customer should choose you instead of your competitors, is an important element in the mission statement. It will determine your attitude and language throughout the planning or your marketing process.

Plans, goals, mission statements, and strategies can change over the life of your business. But if you don't have these things to guide you, you're just like Alice, wondering which road to take. A business without plans, goals or a mission will consume your life's savings or its own value.

With a mission statement and the management of all five of the building blocks of marketing, you will establish the continuity necessary to gain your customers' trust and business. Even if your business operates on a shoestring, with careful planning, you will know which road to take.

Chapter 2

Market Research

If you were a gambler, and you knew of a way to improve your odds of winning by doing some advance research, wouldn't you invest some time?

That's exactly what market research is, a way to help improve your odds of success. Whether you are launching a new business, a new product, or a new product for your existing business, market research will greatly improve your odds of success.

Don't get nervous, market research doesn't have to be highly technical. What you want from your market research is a clear picture of who's out there, both in terms of potential customers and potential competitors. You'll want to identify your position in the market place as compared to your competitors and as your customers see you. Most of your market research can be accomplished by walking through your neighborhood, studying the Yellow Pages, and talking to people you already know.

Market research should look at two categories:

Potential Customers
Potential Competitors

Potential customers

The tendency of many small business owners is to try to be all things to all people. Most successful businesses have found that zeroing in on a target customer is a better way.

The more focused you are on specific types of customers, the easier it is to find them and sell to them.

Customers can be identified in a number of categories. Most businesses identify their customers by demographics and use categories such as age, income level, and family status. You may also identify your target customers by lifestyles, hobbies, common problems (that you solve), geographic location, and buying habits, for example.

New product or business

If yours is a new product or business, market research will help you determine whether your product or service idea is a good one, where you should locate your business to make yourself accessible to the people most likely to buy it, and whether it's even a good idea to go into full-scale production.

Market research doesn't always give you good news. You may have a great idea for a new product, but if there's no one to buy it, you should know this before you go into production.

You'll first want to identify who your product or service is designed for. The more you can focus on a particular kind of person, the easier and more accurate your market research will be.

Let's say you've come up with a new idea for men's dress shoes that are impervious to the elements, yet look like the finest leather available. You would first want to decide who could benefit by owning a pair of these shoes. Certainly business men who travel on business regularly would be interested, particularly those who make many trips through rental car parking lots in the Midwest in January!

Having identified the business traveler as your target customer for this product, the next step is to talk to some business travelers and ask them if they would buy your product.

Business location

Before you open a new business, or a branch of an existing business, market research is equally important.

Having taken the important step of identifying your target customers, it's a simple process to find out if there is a sufficient number of them living in a specific area. Demographic information is as close as your public library. A good first step is to sit down with the U.S. Statistical Abstract. This Commerce Department document provides all kinds of information on the population, broken down by market areas. The U.S. Census also provides information on the population, including home ownership, density, and ages of residents.

Test marketing

You may want to produce a small quantity of your new product for test marketing before going into full-scale production. Typically, your cost per unit will be higher in the small run, but your total investment can be reasonable.

What you want to do is get your product into the hands of people who are likely to benefit from using it to find out how they like it. This test can be as large or as small as you want to make it. Remember, the more people who try your product during the testing period, the more information you will have to work with.

The information is also more likely to be objective. It may seem to make sense to give test versions of your product to a handful of friends to get their opinions. But will they be as honest with you as total strangers would be? You don't just want good news from this test. You want to know if people will really buy your product, and if it really does what you've designed it to do.

National manufacturers test market new products in one or more of the cities they have identified as typical markets. They consider these test markets to be microcosms of the national market because the demographic mix matches that of the country overall. They offer and promote the new product in those markets to test consumer reception. If the product takes off in these representative markets, the odds are good that it will work at the national level.

You can do the same thing on a smaller scale. If you have developed a new product, you may get a few local stores to test market the product for you.

The point is, you don't want to go into full-scale production unless it's likely the product is going to sell. A smaller investment in good market research can save you from a big loss.

The competition

Unless you have a product that is absolutely unique in all the world, you are not going to be the only one competing for your target customer group.

Generally, each of your competitors will fall into one of these three categories:

Market Leader

Challenger

Follower

The Market Leader is easy to identify. The market leader is the one that you want to be when you "grow up." The leader is the trend-setter, at least in its market. All other competitors compare themselves to the leader, and so will you.

There may be several challengers in your market. The challenger admits that the leader is the leader, and is constantly nipping at its heels. Often, challengers compare themselves openly to the leader in advertising, pointing out their own strengths against the leader's weaknesses.

The national car rental companies offer a perfect example of a leader and a challenger. Hertz advertises itself as "Number 1," while Avis says, "We're Number Two, We Try Harder."

Followers generally compete with the leader indirectly, focusing on one area of differentiation such as price, convenience, or some other specific area. Sticking with the car rental companies, it's easy to name three or four followers in the industry. They basically try to do the same things the leader does, offering the buying public a less expensive alternative.

Your market position

Part of reason for market research is to determine what your market strategy will be. Each market position indicates a specific strategy. When you know your market position, it will dictate your areas of competitive advantage and disadvantage, your language in your advertising, and the image you'll portray.

There is usually only one real market leader. Unless you happen to be in that position, don't act like you are. The public already knows who the leader is.

The choice of a challenger strategy is a decision to go head-to-head with the market leader. This strategy will take resources similar to those the leader expends in advertising and promotion. Unless you have the budget to promote your business on a scale similar to that of the leader's, you won't want to pursue the challenger strategy.

The follower strategy is easy. You just try to do most of the things the leader does. Your competitive advantage isn't going to make you stand out in the market place because you're really not all that different! The motto of the follower is: "There's plenty of business out there for all of us." Followers don't enjoy the customer loyalty the leader does, so they're most affected when new competitors come to town. The follower strategy is not recommended for small businesses because there's a strategy that's better and this is the "Nicher" strategy.

The Nicher finds a unique way to serve a specific customer. Often the Nicher serves a market segment that would either be insignificant to the leader, or impractical for the leader to pursue. Using the rental car example, there are companies who rent exotic cars like Rolls Royces and Ferarris. There is a very small market segment that is likely to rent such cars, and the risk and expense of owning and renting such cars is considerable. It just doesn't fit in with Hertz' strategy, nor its challengers' and their followers' strategies, to compete in the exotic car market.

The niche marketer is marketing to a small market segment, providing products and services that are unavailable elsewhere. The niche marketer is less affected by price competition, because they have few competitors that buyers can compare them to.

The Nicher, in effect, establishes itself as the market leader in a very small and specific market. If a new competitor comes after the same niche, it will have the first Nicher's leader position to contend with.

Invest the time to determine who your target customer is, and who you will have to compete with, to bring that customer to your door. This information will affect everything you do in your business.

Chapter 3

Product Development

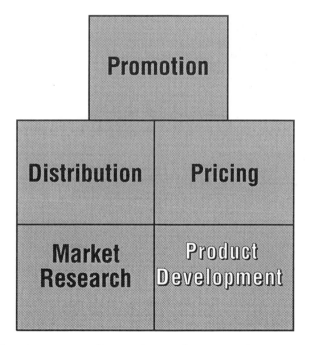

Developing your line of products and services is a balancing act. Notice the relationship between the blocks of product development and market research and think of their relationship in terms of the "Chicken and the Egg."

Your product must satisfy a specific customer, and there must be enough of these customers out there to buy it. So, do you design the product first, then identify a market? Or, do you identify a market, and design a product to satisfy it?

Whether you are planning to sell a product that you have designed, a product that you buy from the manufacturer and resell, or a service, there are some important decisions you must face before you open your doors.

Product development is the process of designing or adopting products and services that you can make valuable enough to buyers so that they will buy these products from you.

If you are reselling a product, you will also determine how you will add value to it. Why should the customer buy it from you instead of directly from the manufacturer?

If you are selling a service, what are its characteristics, or features, and what are the benefits provided to the buyer?

Your own product must somehow be different from any other on the market. What makes it different? Why should the customer buy yours instead of the other competitive products?

Product development answers these questions and depends for strong market research. That's why the two components are the very foundation of the five building blocks.

One major decision is just how many products or services you will offer.

Your overall market strategy helps determine how many products and how broad a product line you'll offer.

Product mix

The mix in your product line has two dimensions, *width* and *depth*.

"Mix width" is the number of different products you'll offer. How diversified is your product line? The more you specialize, the less variety you'll have in your product line. Referring to the example of the cookware store, its width is limited to items that are used in the kitchen. That limited width is what makes it a specialist.

"Mix depth" is the number of different models, manufacturers, or styles you'll offer among the products in your width. If you sell cookware, how many lines of kitchen knives will you carry?

There are even stores that take this specialty to the level of offering only knives, a very narrow mix width. But they offer knives from many manufactures, for many uses, and in a broad range of prices. If you're in the market for any kind of a knife, you'll find what you need here. This is a very deep mix.

A business may offer a large number of different products, but only one option for each product offered. Convenience stores may offer everything from motor oil, to groceries, to underwear, creating a broad mix width. But customers have only one brand of each item to choose from. The convenience store's specialty is its broad width.

You can fill a lot of needs at a convenience store, usually 24-hours-a-day, but you're not going to find much selection. In this example, consumers give up price and selection in exchange for convenience.

Huge department stores position themselves with "selection," meaning broad width and depth. Department stores offer lots of different products and a number of different manufacturers' products in each department.

Successful small businesses limit either mix width or mix depth as a point of differentiation from competitors.

As you add new products and services, you affect either mix width or your mix depth. It's generally better to limit yourself consistently in one dimension or the other. In other words, don't add significantly to depth in one product line when your broad mix width (or selection) is your differentiation point.

New product development

There will be times when you consider adding new products to your line, either as part of a growth strategy, or as a way of maintaining your current position.

Depending on what kind of business you are in, this may mean invention and development of new product ideas, or improvement of existing products. If you are reselling products developed and produced by other suppliers, it actually means *product selection*.

Many businesses were started because their owners had a "better mouse trap" idea. Unfortunately, statistics show that more than 90 percent of new product ideas fail. Sometimes, it's just because the mousetrap was not better. It may have been a good idea, but one that just didn't serve enough people to make money. In most cases, however, new products fail because the inventor failed to make product development one of five building blocks. Instead, the entrepreneur may have assumed: "If you build a better mousetrap, customers will beat a path to your door."

Since the five building blocks are interdependent, all five must be clearly thought out if your product is going to be successful. When it comes to product development, your purpose is to confirm that the products that you sell will do something for the buyer.

Maybe your new product provides some level of pleasure, security, or comfort that the customer can't get from other products in the market place.

Are you solving a problem that no other product solves? You may have found a new solution that is faster, easier, or less expensive than those of other products that are available.

As you can see, as you work on product development, pricing is an issue that comes into play as well. All five of the blocks are interdependent.

Product differentiation

If there is nothing about your product or service that makes it different from the ones offered by competitors, the customer will have no reason to buy from you.

If indeed you have developed a "better mousetrap," what makes it better? For your product to be "better" in the eyes of the consumer, it must satisfy the consumer with one of these differentiation points:

Price: *Is your new mousetrap less expensive?*

Convenience: *Is it easier to use, or more readily available?*

Service: *Do you come in and pick up the trap after it has "worked" so the consumer doesn't have to?*

Selection: *Does it come in a variety of styles, sizes or colors?*

Quality: *Will it last longer, or do its job better?*

Trust: *Do you have a reputation that engenders trust?*

Loyalty: *Are your customers so loyal they'll buy from you just because they like to do business with you?*

Dependability: *Is yours a "sure-kill" mousetrap?*

There are other differentiation points, but these are the most common.

As you develop or select your product line, look at it from the eyes of the intended consumer. If you cannot identify a key difference that translates into an advantage over your competitors' offerings, it's not likely to fly!

Make sure your differentiation point is one that you can defend. If you use price as a differentiation point, are you sure that competitors won't match your price, taking away the differentiation?

Testing

Of course, before you build a production facility for a new product, you want to be pretty confident that it's going to fly. You'll want to do something before you go into full scale production to make sure the product can make money.

Even if you're reselling a supplier's product, you should determine the strength of its differentiation points before you buy a big inventory, or devote resources to a large scale promotion or display.

Smart marketers test new offerings by making them available on a limited scale, to those they consider to be a typical group of buyers fitting their target customer profile.

National marketers have identified cities where they have experienced consumer buying habits that match their national average. They will make a new product available in several of these markets for a limited period to test the market's response.

This is why you may find different items available at national fast food outlets when you travel. That item that you don't see in your city is being tested. If it succeeds in the test market, it will be made available nationally. If not, you'll probably never see it again.

On a smaller scale, you may have a party to whom you wish to introduce the new product or service that you're considering. You can invite customers and prospects from your list who are "typical" customers. If their reaction is positive, it's probably worth a try.

This can even be as simple as surveying your current customers to find out if there is demand for the new product. Many businesses survey customers regularly to monitor service and quality levels.

When testing with current customers, remember that they already know and trust you. Unless current customers are the only intended market for the new product, it's important to identify differentiation points that will appeal to the rest of your intended market.

Current customers are your likeliest prospects. If they don't buy it, it's unlikely total strangers will.

As stressed earlier, everything you do depends on your target customer. The products you sell, and the price you charge, will depend on the customer's perception of your products and services as compared to those offered by your competitors.

So you see, the issues of product development and market research go hand in hand. No matter how good the product idea is (based on product development), there has to be a sufficient number of buyers (based on market research) willing to pay a profitable price (based on pricing—the next chapter) if you are to succeed.

Chapter 4

Pricing

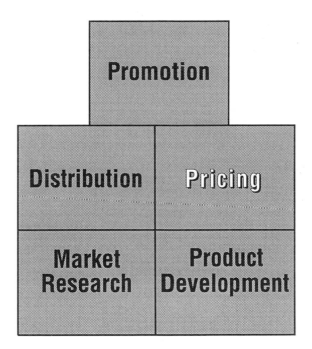

No matter what product or service you provide, pricing decisions may well be the most difficult you make.

You're going to have to answer these important questions:

1. Is my target customer willing and able to pay the price?

2. Is my price competitive in the market?

3. Am I pricing my product so that I can make a profit?

4. Where does this individual product or service fit in to my overall pricing and profit strategy?

The customer

Let's start with the most important person in the process—the customer. Even though a number of factors come into play, none is more important than realizing what your product or service is worth to your customer. You have to look at two dimensions of the buyer's decision: why the customer is buying the product and why the customer selected the particular product or seller.

Why does a customer buy a product or service to begin with? The buyer's original motivation to buy falls into one of these five categories:

Utility— things I have to have to survive;

Luxury—things I would like to have (discretionary money);

Impulse—snap decisions (some people buy a cars on impulse!);

Emergency—short term necessity—no choice but to buy.

To make it even more complicated, one buyer's utility item is another's luxury. Pricing is affected by what part of the budget the money comes from. Is this item included in the monthly budget, or is it likely to be bought with discretionary cash?

One customer may have to own a car to commute to work. That customer's buying motivation is utility and the money comes from the monthly budget.

Another customer may buy a car as a luxury item and would therefore buy it with discretionary cash.

Ask anyone who sells cars, and he or she will tell you that many are bought on impulse. The buyer was there to have the old car serviced, and just fell in love with a car in the showroom.

If you need a car for your work and it's wrecked in an accident, you may buy a car as an emergency item.

Impulse and emergency items may cause the buyer to alter the monthly budget to accommodate the purchase.

You have to know what usually motivates your target customer, and price accordingly. Again, that issue of clearly identifying your target customer comes into play.

The market

The second consideration is whether your prices are competitive in the market.

Part of market research was knowing who your top competitors are, and what your advantage is over each. This knowledge now comes into play in the pricing decision.

Earlier, you asked yourself the question, "Why should the customer choose my business?" In pricing your products and services, you must consider how your products and services differ from your competitors'.

As you'll remember from Chapter 3, customers may base their buying decision on any of these differentiation points: price, convenience, service, selection, quality, trust, loyalty, dependability. How much you provide of each of these affects the value your customer receives.

If your price is higher than your competitor's price for a similar product, you must add value to justify the price. That extra value may be in the product itself. If your product is of higher quality than the competitor's comparable product, that is your differentiation point.

You may sell exactly the same product as a competitor. What do you do to add value to yours? If your price is the same, but you are more convenient to the customer, you get the sale. If you are a lot more convenient, you may even be able to charge a higher price than the competitor.

Profitability

Don't base your pricing decisions entirely on the competition and the market. If you aren't profitable, you won't be around for long.

The basic pricing formula is:

Cost of Goods Sold (COGS) + Markup = Price.

Be sure to calculate the cost of goods sold carefully. For example, you may buy your product from a manufacturer or distributor, then resell it to your customers. In this case, the price you pay the factory or distributor is just the beginning of your actual cost. For each product you sell, you must allocate a share of your overall expenses to the cost of selling that product.

Allocating expenses to each product should be done carefully. For instance, when allocating a fair share of your rent and utilities to a product's COGS, you have to consider how many square feet are used to store the inventory. What percentage of your sales force's time is spent promoting this product. Distribution costs, transportation, storage and display, add to the COGS. Include advertising, travel expenses, office supplies, etc.

Use the table on the following page as a model and change the categories where necessary to include your specific costs. Then you'll have a template that makes sure you capture all of your costs each time you have to calculate. You can see this is a perfect application for your computer spreadsheet. Math errors do happen with manual calculations. The computer spreadsheet ensures accurate and complete calculations.

ITEM	Labor	Materials	Overhead	Shipping	Storage	Display	TOTAL
Capital							
Markup							

One expense that is often forgotten in this calculation is the cost of capital. You have money tied up in your inventory, whether you borrowed it or invested your own cash.

If your cash is tied up in inventory, it is no longer earning interest or growing in other investments. That loss of interest or potential growth is your cost of capital. If your inventory is paid for with borrowed money, or "floor planned," the interest you pay is your cost of capital.

Also include your cost of extending credit. If you are giving customers 90 days to pay, that's 90 days that the capital is tied up or costing you interest.

The cost of capital can be significant, and must be considered in the COGS calculation.

Markup

Your price has to cover that Cost of Goods Sold, plus a markup. Now is when you'll consider how much the customer is willing to pay, and how you will deal with the competition.

If you cannot charge customers enough to cover your cost of goods sold, either because of their price resistance or because a competitor is offering a price lower than your COGS, you have some tough choices to make.

Never price a product below your Cost of Goods Sold unless it is part of a specific strategy to attract customers who will also buy a highly profitable product. This is called the "loss leader" strategy. You see supermarkets battle for the lowest price on turkeys at Thanksgiving time. The strategy is to get customers into the store and entice them to buy all the (profitable) trimmings at the same time.

In most cases, you'll want to find a way to either add value to your product, so the customer will pay the higher price, or to lower your COGS, leaving room for a markup.

We already talked about adding value. Some of the ways you add value will also add to your COGS, and you must take these into consideration. For instance, if you stay open later or offer free delivery to provide added convenience, you will add to your COGS.

If you add value by providing better service, you probably don't add significantly to your cost, unless you pay for an extensive customer service training program for your employees.

If service is your differentiation point, does the customer see it that way? Remember, if it doesn't represent significant value to the customer, it just doesn't matter!

Price is actually well down on the list of reasons customers buy from one supplier instead of another. Don't assume that your price has to be lower than your competitor's. Just understand that the customer has to perceive he or she is receiving more value from you to be willing to pay the higher price.

Overall product/price strategy

As discussed in the chapter on product development, most businesses have a mix of products and services. As you price each one, understand that you will have different levels of profitability for each.

Referring again to the example of the Thanksgiving turkey, identify where each of your products falls in your "food chain."

Anchor	Cash Cow
Trial Balloon	Extra
Loser	Loss Leader

The grocery stores offer Turkeys at the holidays at prices at or below their actual cost for the product. They do that to attract customers to the store, in hopes that they will buy all of the ingredients for the dinner. That is called a *loss leader* price strategy. The retailer is willing to lose money on that transaction, in exchange for the larger, more profitable sale.

You may have some products that are just plain losers; they don't make you money, but you may feel that you have to carry them to maintain your customers. Or you may subscribe to the theory that: "I lose money every time I make a sale, but I hope to make it up on volume." Of course, selling a higher volume of losers will just lose more money. Either raise the price of loser items so you break even, or get them out of your product line.

Trial balloons are new products that you price at a level that will build interest. When you add new products to your line, the trial balloon price should be at least marginally profitable. A 10 to 20 percent markup over your cost of goods sold would be typical of most retail trial balloons. If the product is a success, you can then place it into one of the remaining price categories.

By the way, any time you place a product on "sale," you will probably work in the trial balloon price range, unless it is a clearance sale. You may reduce a popular, profitable product to a trial balloon level temporarily to generate new interest in the product.

Extras are products that sell as add-ons to other purchases. You may have a loss leader product, but sell extras to almost everyone who comes in for the loss leader. The products priced as extras must, therefore, be priced with a higher profit margin than the trial balloon. A markup of 25 to 50 percent is appropriate for an extra. Remember, it must make up for the loss leader product with which it goes out the door.

Anchors are those products that represent the bulk of your business. Many businesses have only a few anchor products, and several extras to go with them. Products priced as anchors must be the mainstay of your product line. They are what your business is known for.

The anchor price level should be very profitable. Depending on what business you're in, anchor products can carry markups of 25 to 100 percent.

Cash cows are products that are in such demand that you can price them at premium levels. Since the laws of supply and demand still apply, items in high demand but low in availability are priced as cash cows. Unique products that take off in the market are often priced as cash cows.

Markups of more than 100 percent of cost of goods sold are not uncommon with these products.

Not everyone has a cash cow in their line. Of course, everyone would like to have one, but don't feel bad if you don't. Even if you have one, it's likely your competitors are working on a way to offer the same or a nearly identical product at a lower price, which will force you to lower your price.

Chapter 5

Distribution

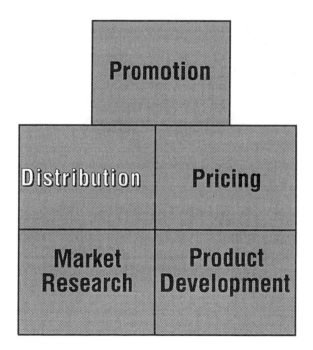

How goods and services physically move from the producer to the end user is a key marketing consideration. The details of distribution are not the most glamorous activities, but they directly impact the other four building blocks.

Many businesses have considered distribution as an afterthought. If you leave distribution considerations for last, or worse—after advertising and promotion have started, you run the risk of being unable to deliver your product to your customer.

The logistics involved in distribution include the physical movement and handling of your product between the time it is produced and the time the customer takes possession.

The distribution chain may include any or all of these links:

Manufacturer   Transportation   Retailer   Transportation   Consumer

Distributors or wholesalers may also be in the chain. Warehouse or backroom storage may be required at one or several points in the process. At each stage in the process, the product will be in one of three physical states: storage, transportation, and display. Each link in the chain adds to the cost of the product, the risk of delay, and the risk of loss or damage.

After the product is produced, the manufacturer will store it, either on its premises or at a warehouse, until it is shipped to the first buyer in the distribution chain. That buyer may be a distributor or wholesaler, who will then store the product on its premises until it is shipped to the retail outlet. The product is then stored, and/or displayed by the retailer until the end user buys it. The retailer will probably display at least one sample of the product so that consumers can see what it looks like, possibly operate the sample, and make their buying decision. The product is then transported to the consumer's premises, either by the retailer or a delivery service, or by the consumer.

In your business, some of these steps may be bypassed. Each step that is bypassed reduces the cost of the product, the time from production to end user, and the risks of loss or damage.

Many products are marketed as "factory direct," meaning the manufacturer sells directly to the end user. If the consumer visits a factory showroom, buys the product on the spot, and takes it home, all of the transportation costs, risks and delays, and most of the storage costs and risks, are eliminated.

Your place in the distribution chain

Where you fit into this chain, and how you deal with the logistics of storage, transportation and display, are important considerations.

If you are a retailer, you may well have to deal with all three of these physical considerations. How you handle each aspect will affect your cost of goods sold, and therefore, the price you'll charge.

These considerations will also affect your selection of suppliers. If two suppliers offer the same product, but one is across town while the other is across the country, the difference in transportation costs will make the local supplier more desirable. The local supplier can also get the product to you faster, which may mean you can reduce the inventory that you have to store on your own premises, reducing your storage expense and risk.

Transportation

In order to control transportation factors, you will want to consider the cost, risk, and the time involved in each leg of your product's journey. Selecting the mode of transportation, and the actual carrier, can be confusing and difficult.

Generally, as you reduce cost, you'll probably be increasing the time factor. Transportation of perishable products that require refrigeration is more expensive than transporting hard goods.

The size of your shipments also affects the transportation costs. The cost of transporting a rail car full of your product will be relatively low. However, moving goods by rail is generally one of the slower ways to transport, so you'll probably have to order well in advance of inventory depletion. You'll also spend some of the money saved on transportation for storage of the large quantity when it is delivered, and on the capital that is tied up in the large order.

Of course, most retailers don't buy inventory by the train load.

The rule of thumb is: the greater the quantity of product you order in each shipment, the lower the transportation cost per unit will be; and, the slower the mode of transportation, the lower the transportation cost.

Storage

Once you take delivery of the product, you will have to provide a safe place to store it. The product in storage (and on display) on your premises is your inventory.

You'll want to manage your inventory so that you never run out of any item. After all, you don't want to spend more on storage and insurance costs than you saved by ordering large shipments.

Therefore, the portion of your rent that pays for inventory storage space should be considered as part of your cost of distribution.

Also adding considerably to your distribution costs is the risk involved in storage. That inventory is exposed to the danger of fire and theft and must be insured adequately.

You also have the less tangible risk of being overstocked. It is possible to buy more of a particular product than you can sell in a reasonable amount of time. The inventory has to turn over regularly, or you may be left with obsolete units and the cost of tying up capital in the inventory may erode your profits.

Profit on most products depends largely on turnover: How many units can you move each month? If you don't have units in stock, it may be more difficult to move large numbers. On the other hand, if your costs of storing, shipping and financing the inventory add too much to the price and make it unattractive, it may be difficult to sell those units.

Display

Your role in the distribution process includes making it easy for the consumer to buy and obtain the product. How the product is made available to the consumer can greatly affect its attractiveness. From the consumers' point of view, availability includes where they have to go to see the product, the hours your business is open and the ease with which they can take the product home.

The space occupied by display, plus the cost of decorating the showroom or display area, must be included in the distribution strategy and costs. This is where the goods move from producer to consumer. It is next to the last step in the distribution process. After the consumer makes the purchase, the last step is delivery.

Therefore, the product sample has to be in a place that is convenient for the consumer to see it and to arrange for delivery. Delivery may mean that the consumer carries it home or arranges for delivery by the retailer.

You can see how the warehouse market operations can offer lower prices. They buy large quantities, obtain bulk prices and save on transportation costs. The effective use of vertical space creates inexpensive storage for large quantities. Warehouse-style stores don't spend a lot of money and space on displaying products. The consumer carries the product out the door so there is no delivery cost other than the cost of bringing shopping carts back in from the parking lot.

These stores do, of course, have lots of capital tied up in inventory. However, they manage to turn their inventory over often, which is where their profit lies—low costs and markups per unit, but lots of units moved!

If customers are to be persuaded by your display, your business must be convenient and easy to find. Your business' location and hours of operation are also important functions of your ability to deliver to the customer.

Whether you are in a product or a service-oriented business, making it easy for the customer to do business with you is crucial to your success.

Location

The location of your target customer determines where you can locate your business. If yours is a retail business where customers demand to touch the product before they buy it, you must locate where it is easy for them to come in and shop.

Your business should be easy to find and easy to visit.

To be easy to find, you should try to locate in a place that requires only simple directions. This is why space at major intersections is expensive. It's easy to find, and easy to access. Since there are only so many major intersections, malls were developed to create a landmark for their tenants. Your location is easy to find when all the customer needs is the name of a major mall.

Another advantage of mall locations is the availability of parking. The types of businesses that have "short stop" customers who merely stop to drop off or pick up items will prefer strip mall locations. Parking is usually available within steps of the front door. It would be inconvenient for a dry cleaner's customers to drop and pick up orders inside a large shopping mall. A Main Street location with no easy drive-up or dedicated parking would also be inconvenient for that kind of business.

If your customers have time for shopping, and are likely to spend time browsing and window shopping, an enclosed mall or Main Street location may be excellent.

Hours

Your business hours are a major marketing decision. Are you available at the time of day (or days of the week) that is convenient for your target customer?

Take a look at your customers' schedules. If your target customer is the two-income family with children, you can be certain they're busy people. Your hours have to make you available when they're available.

If your competitor's phone lines are open 24 hours a day, 7 days a week, while you're only open 9 to 5, Monday through Friday, then your competitor's got the advantage.

The reason Automated Teller Machines (ATMs) have become integral to the banking industry's distribution system is their around-the-clock availability. Consumers didn't adopt them simply because they loved the new technology. More importantly, ATMs enabled consumers to adhere to their own schedules. Distribution must be designed to make the flow from manufacturer to end user timely, efficient, convenient, and cost-efficient. It's an important building block in your marketing plan.

Chapter 6

Promotion

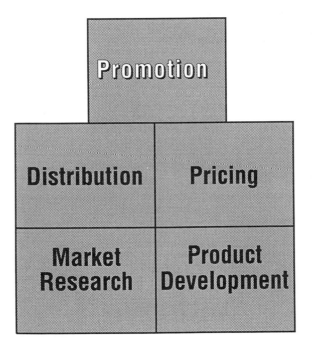

Promotion is the last of the marketing building blocks to be discussed for a good reason.

Many business owners make the mistake of jumping into promotional activities before they have made the key marketing decisions that should guide their promotional efforts. Only after the first four building blocks have been put into place should you think about promotion.

As a small business owner, your promotional budget is likely on a shoestring. Therefore, it is imperative that you spend your time and money efficiently. You don't have to have a huge budget to make an impact. But you do have to direct your message carefully to the audience you have identified as your target customers, without spending a lot of money on *overflow* advertising.

Any advertising that is read by large numbers of people who will never do business with you is overflow. In this book, advertising media that go directly to your target customer with a minimum of overflow is featured.

This book intentionally avoids a discussion of broadcast media like radio and television. Although the TV and radio advertising sales representatives will tell you that they have carefully identified their audience in demographic terms, you will still be paying for considerable overflow.

The term "broadcast" is clearly incompatible with the term "target." Small businesses simply can't afford to broadcast their message.

To market effectively on a shoestring budget, you must identify your target customers, design a line of products and services especially for them, and find a way to place your message directly in their eyes. Broadcast media simply reach too many people. Generally, you will be paying for coverage beyond your means.

The promotional media recommended in this book are designed to reach your target customer and only your target customer. Only no-cost methods are used to add new names to your contact lists. This way, all of your promotional dollars are spent talking directly to real prospects without wasting money on overflow.

The business world is evolving away from being a mass-production environment. The new businesses that will succeed in the coming millennium will be tuned into their customers as individuals.

New developments in computers, robotics and communications enable businesses to create products and services that are customized. Even golf clubs are now custom fitted, as opposed to the "one size fits all" clubs of just a few years ago.

A laser system now measures the customer and to create a custom-fitted suit. This is not a mass-produced suit that is altered to fit; it is a suit sewn from fabric the customer selects, using the precision measurements taken by the laser beam.

Access to the internet enables consumers to learn more than many sales people know about products they are considering. This educated customer knows exactly what he or she wants, and will only do business with the organization that can provide it.

In this environment, you can't hope to be all things to all people. The more your business focuses on a specific type of individual, the more effectively you'll market to him or her. You may reach those individuals by broadcasting your message, but there are guaranteed methods to address those individuals directly.

The chapter on direct mail is the longest chapter in this book because direct mail is the most effective of the low-cost marketing media. Direct mail is a perfect example of the way successful businesses in the new millennium will deal with their customers. You can place your message directly into the hands of the individual you want to read it. If you have done your market research and developed products that serve the individuals on your mailing list, your odds of making a sale are pretty good, aren't they?

The names you place on your mailing list should be found through no-cost media. Networking and public speaking will be your media for developing leads. You don't want to spend money to talk to people unless you know they are real prospects for the product or service you are promoting.

Mailing to addresses from a rented list is broadcasting. The very best of direct mail advertisers expect responses from two or three percent of their mail recipients. Mailing to anyone you don't already know, and who doesn't already know about you is not recommended.

Think of promotion as "courting." There must be a relationship with the individual if the courtship is going to reach fruition. You must consistently present products and services that the "courtee" is predisposed to buying, in a price range that is attractive. You must only court those to whom you are easily available (distribution), and who already know and trust you.

As you can see, the first four building blocks of marketing, market research, product development, distribution, and pricing provide the foundation for the fifth—promotion.

Market research determines to whom will promote. The identification of your target customers, the people most likely to buy you product or service, is key to all of your promotion decisions. It determines what media you will use to reach these people. It determines the *reach*, or number of people, you will be trying to contact with your promotions.

Repetition is important to the success of your advertising and promotion. The consumer must see your message six or seven times to remember it. Working within the confines of a shoestring budget means you will undoubtedly have to limit the number of people you promote yourself to (reach) in order to make a number of impressions (repetition) within a reasonable amount of time.

If you don't contact your customers and prospects at least half a dozen times each year, they may well forget you. Monthly contact is preferred to be sure you keep in touch. That may mean reducing the number of names on your list. Contacting 1,000 people 12 times in a year will definitely get you more results than contacting 4,000 people three times.

It's tempting to try to reach the masses, but you will establish stronger relationships with your customers if you focus on the smaller numbers.

Whether the customer you've identified as your target customer is willing to pay the price for your product, and how the customer will obtain it, all have to be determined before you ever start designing advertising and promotion strategies.

The chapters that follow give you ideas and instruction in the most economical yet effective media to reach new prospects, turn them into customers, and keep business coming from your current customers.

Concentrate your promotional efforts on your real prospects, and people who already do business with you. Everyone else is overflow, and you don't need to waste any of your precious promotional dollars talking to them.

Chapter 7

Networking

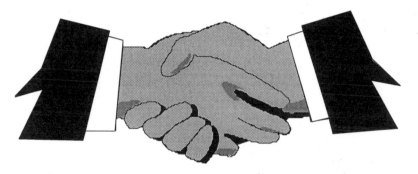

net•work (net′wûrk′) n. 1. an interconnected
system, a network of alliances

net•work v. 1. to make connections among people
or groups.

The least expensive marketing technique also
happens to be the most effective for small businesses!
Networking costs you nothing but your time, and the
return on this investment can be enormous. You do
have to approach this as you would any other
marketing activity—you have to plan in advance.

It's best to start your networking campaign with specific goals.

Networking goals center around adding people to your network. For example, one goal might be to add five new people per week to your network. How hard is that? If you do that, you'll add 60 people per year to your list of human resources.

As you meet people and consider adding them to your network, don't necessarily concentrate only on the people who are potential customers. Remember that everyone you meet has a network of friends and business associates, members of which may be prospects for your own. Think of yourself as developing a circle of influence, not just a list of prospects.

Reciprocity

Likewise, in networking, you are making yourself available for friends' and aquaintances' lists of resources. It's important to realize that networking is a two-way street. Webster's dictionary defines the noun *network* as an interconnected system.

Effective networkers know that the people in any network depend on one another. Therefore, your goals should include assisting your contacts in your network. One of the most important lessons in this writer's career is that everything you do for others has an effect that comes back to you. You can't always trace that effect clearly and not every favor is returned directly. Not everyone networks as unselfishly as you do. However, helping others is the key to receiving, in business and in life.

Follow-up should be included in your networking goals. Plan to follow-up in response to ten people per week. Follow-up may mean a quick phone call just to say "hello" or to pass on a tip you think would be beneficial to your contact.

In the magazines and books you read, watch for information and stories that you can pass on to people in your network. Photocopy articles or pages and drop them in the mail or fax them to the people who would be interested.

Keeping track

This brings up an important step in the networking process. Devise some way to keep track of your network, and to break the list down by interests or professions, and keep in touch.

This group deserves personal contact, not mass mailings. Hand written notes or phone calls are much more appropriate than computer generated letters. Don't insult people with "personal" correspondence that looks like it went to 100 others as well.

To organize your network, you can create a sort of family tree. Start with your name in the center of a piece of paper. Then, draw a line in one direction listing everyone in your same type of business. Another line may list relatives. Then draw lines for your golfing partners, the members of your Rotary club, and so forth.

You may have a branch that lists people who work in human resources and another that lists small business owners. Some people may appear on more than one branch.

There are several excellent computer programs on the market that are designed specifically for network management. The point is to be able to see who you can share specific information with at a glance.

One final recommendation as a goal is to introduce five people in your network to each other each week. Make a point of helping others expand their networks, and they will naturally introduce you to their associates.

A great way to make introductions is to invite a guest to every meeting of the organizations to which you belong. This gives your contacts a chance to meet new people and they will often reciprocate by inviting you to one of their meetings.

Where to network

You already belong to clubs, religious organizations, business associations, and similar structured groups. At their meetings, you should be looking for opportunities to meet new people, to maintain or rekindle existing relationships, and to help the people in your network meet each other.

Remember these three objectives. You are always expanding your network without turning your back on the people who are already in your network. Linking people within your network is sharing the wealth of your resources and this sharing makes your network even stronger.

Every time you meet someone new, on the golf course or at a business meeting, you should consider his or her network potential. If you're uncomfortable with this idea, it's because you're not thinking from a giving perspective. When you think of networking in terms of constantly looking for opportunities to help others in their business or personal lives, networking takes on a different image.

Meeting people

OK, you've taken the plunge. You're at your local Chamber of Commerce meeting with the objective of building your network. As you look around, it will become apparent that most others are there for the same reason. However, many will be unsuccessful in their efforts because they don't know how to get started.

Step one is to meet people. The natural tendency is to stay in conversational circles with people you already know. Although it is important to maintain these relationships, it's also important to expand your network. You can either venture off on your own to meet new people or you can invite new people to join your circle.

If you see someone standing alone, walk up and introduce yourself. So, what do you say?

The introduction

Experienced networks are good at introducing themselves in a way that tells something about themselves and encourages the other party to tell a little about him or herself.

If you're not used to being that forward, take some time to rehearse a good introduction. Keep it simple: "Hi, I'm Larry Mersereau, I'm the club treasurer."

Or say something about the room or the occasion. Make positive comments and tack on an open-ended question. "What a great turn out! What's your connection with this group?"

The handshake

Physical touch is one of the strongest human bonding agents. In any situation, the handshake is accepted as a safe way to establish that physical bond.

A good handshake is firm, confident and "web to web." The little web that connects your thumb to your first finger should be placed directly against the other party's web. This is the right depth for the handshake.

Make eye contact a part of the handshake because it reinforces the physical connection.

Hold the handshake just long enough to make a solid connection. Don't linger too long or the other party will become uncomfortable.

The conversation

Successful networkers don't come to meetings to sell. They come to meet new people, add names to their network and think not what they can do for themselves, but what they can do for others.

People love to talk about themselves. Your conversation should give other people the opportunity to do this. Consequently, you'll have the opportunity to learn about them, their businesses, and what you can do to help them. Don't be afraid to ask direct questions like, "What kind of people do business with you?" or "What would a good lead be for you?"

Business cards

Your goal is not to see how many business cards you can give away. Instead, your goal is to obtain cards. Offering your card during the course of conversation is really a request to receive the other party's card. As you hand someone your card, say something like, "Please take my card. May I have one of yours?"

Then make notes on the card regarding where he or she fits into the network and what hot buttons you heard during the conversation. Don't assume you will remember this information without jotting it down. If you meet five new people each day, you're not likely to recall all the important data for each person. When you get back to the office, this information will be invaluable as you begin the all-important step of follow-up.

Follow-up

Follow-up relates to what you can do for your contact. Maybe you know someone who would be a good lead for this contact or perhaps you have a magazine article that he or she would find useful.

The point of follow-up is not to ask for business. The purpose of the follow-up is to strengthen your bond with the other person and establish him or her as a member of your network. Make membership in your network as advantageous for your contacts as it is for you.

Chapter 8

Public Speaking

Public speaking is another method of promoting your business that costs you nothing but your time. However, since research suggests that Americans fear public speaking more than death itself, you will probably have to invest a little time in developing your confidence. If you're a nervous presenter, you're not alone. The potential payoff for speaking to groups in your target market is huge. You will be able to reach people that would be difficult and expensive to reach effectively any other way.

Speaking at club and association meetings is a great way to make contact with large numbers of potential clients. Look in your Yellow Pages under both headings, and you'll find a long list of audiences anxious to hear your message.

Virtually every club that meets regularly has a program chairperson who is constantly looking for guest speakers. In major cities, you can speak every day of the year, and never address the same group twice!

Before you offer to speak anywhere, you'll want to make sure the audience is made up of people who fit your target customer profile. Each organization appeals to a specific type of person. If you call the number listed in the Yellow Pages, the club or association representative will gladly tell you about membership characteristics. This may be the easiest market research you ever conduct.

Public speaking provides an opportunity to demonstrate your knowledge and confidence in your product or service. People like to do business with people they know and trust.

Following are some tips to help make the preparation and presentation a little easier and more comfortable.

First of all, it is unnecessary to prepare a totally new and fresh presentation for each and every group. Since you will speak to different groups, the audiences will be new and fresh and one strong presentation can be used over and over.

The second piece of advice is to prepare, prepare! Most nonprofessional speakers spend too little time preparing before their presentation. If you step up to the podium unprepared, you are bound to be nervous. Rehearse your presentation in front of a "speaker-friendly" audience before you present to a group of prospects. "Speaker-friendly" listeners may be family, friends or your staff. Let them tell you what worked in the presentation, and what didn't.

An easy and inexpensive way to improve your speaking skills is to join Toastmasters International. Each club is a group of other business people who are there to improve their communication and leadership skills. There is no more supportive group to speak to anywhere. You'll start small, preparing and presenting short speeches about familiar topics. Using the Toastmasters International workbook, you will go through a series of speeches, each designed to develop a specific set of skills. Podium confidence, voice inflection, and hand gestures are just a few of the skills you'll learn. Each speech is evaluated by a club member based on a criteria sheet in the workbook. You will also critique other members' speeches—a valuable experience as well.

There are Toastmasters Clubs in most cities, usually a number of clubs. Find one that meets at a time when you can attend regularly. The more consistently you attend, the faster you will learn and the more comfortable you'll be in front of any audience.

You've determined which audiences to talk to based on your target market. Now, you'll want to select topics that will both benefit your image and interest your audience.

Audiences are not generally interested in learning about how your product is built or how it functions. They want to know what it does for them.

With this in mind, consider your public speaking as verbal presentations of the same kind of information you would include in advertising copy (see Chapter 11 on direct mail for a fuller discussion of advertising copy). Identify your product's or service's benefits to the user, in this case, your audience. Tell the user how your product or service will improve their lives, make them more profitable or efficient, or solve a specific problem.

If you have a product that you can demonstrate, all the better. "Show and tell" presentations hold an audience's attention much more than straight lectures.

If the audience can handle, or even operate the product, they will remember you even longer.

Chapter 9

DIRECT MAIL

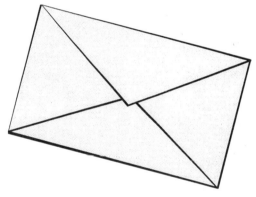

Direct mail is the recommended promotional medium for small businesses. Broadcast media, both electronic and print, talk to entire markets which may or may not include your target customers. The advertising that reaches all those people who are not your target customers is called "overflow" advertising. Broadcast communications include considerable overflow—advertising you pay for knowing there will be no return.

Direct mail speaks to individuals. Only with direct mail can you be sure that the person you want to reach will see your message.

As with all marketing, the most important consideration is your audience. The value of focusing on your specific target customer pays big dividends in direct mail advertising.

By maintaining accurate mailing lists, you spend your advertising dollars speaking directly, and only, to customers and real prospects.

List maintenance

Maintaining your mailing list is clearly a function that lends itself to computerization. There are many programs designed specifically for the job of maintaining your list and integrating the information into labels and letters.

In the table on the next page, you see the outline for a mail list database entry screen. If you are using a computer accounting system, you may already have the capability of generating names based on purchasing history. Don't reinvent the wheel if you already have this capability. With this kind of information, you can mail offers only to the people you know are predisposed to buying. You don't have to mail every offer to every name on your list(s).

Notice the "Occasions" record. The personal touch of sending birthday or anniversary cards will keep you close to your customers. At least make a point of getting this information from your top customers.

Mailing List				
Pre Title:	First Name:		Last Name:	
Company Name:				
Address 1:				
Address 2:				
City:	State:	Zip:	Status:	
Office Phone:		Fax:	Status:	
Marital Status:	Children (y/n):	Sophistication:	Age:	
Buying History		Product		Total Cost
		1:		$1:
		2:		$2:
		3:		$3:
		4:		$4:
Future Interests				
		A:		
		B:		
		C:		
		D:		
Occasions		Name		Occasion
	N1:			O1:
	N2:			O2:
	N3:			O3:
NOTES:				

Special offers may go only to customers you haven't heard from in the past year to reactivate them. Or special rewards may go only to those who have done business with you in the past year. Computers are marvelous tools!

You should at least maintain the following two lists (following each is the general strategy for mailings to them):

- Customers   Customer Retention
  Maintain Contact
  Special Offers
  Highly Targeted Offers
- Prospects   Establish Relationships
  Special Offers
  Maintain Contact

Customers are people who have already done business with you in the past. People who have done business with you in the past are your best source for new business. They know you, they trust you, and they know how to do business with you. You must never let them forget your business; regularly remind them that you are their supplier for whatever it is you sell. If your accounting system can generate labels and letters, you already have a customer list. If not, put together a list in your database or word processing system.

Prospects are people who fit your target customer profile. They're the type of people who should be doing business with you, they just haven't done it yet.

Your objective with the prospect list is to convice them to give your business a try. After a number of mailings, you will establish the recognition we talked about earlier. The rules still apply: convey a consistent message,offer products that fill a need and determine a price range that fits your prospects' comfort zone.

It's important that you select names for the prospect list carefully. If your message, products, and price range are not appropriate, it's a waste of your money to mail to them. This is why adding names to your list culled from the no-cost marketing media like networking and public speaking is so effective—you know these people are real prospects.

Rented Lists

It may be tempting to extend your reach by renting a large list of new names. If this is something you want to do, despite the warnings in this and earlier chapters, there is a specific strategy you should use.

People will not do business with a total stranger unless there is little or no risk to them. The offer to prospects from a rented list must be something that costs them very little or nothing to respond.

You can offer free information, a free sample, or a discounted price for the first item they buy. Research has shown that people are much more likely to try your offer if their risk is less than $10.00. The first item you offer could be a loss leader designed to elicit their response.

Your objective in using a rented mailing list is to elicit responses. You can then add these names to your own list, and keep them in the loop with your customers and other prospects.

It is more expensive to add names to your list this way but with planning, the use of rental lists can still be effective.

All of the elements of a good print advertisement apply to your direct mail message. These include a call to action and a response medium. If the prospective prospect (which is what rented lists give you) is going to respond, you have to get him or her to do it immediately after reading the letter. It must be a compelling, low-risk offer that requires and easy response.

Frequency

Remember the importance of repetition. If the people you mail to are going to remember you, they must see your message six to seven times each year. The question of reasonable reach, how many people you can mail to, comes into play here.

It's really very simple. After you have designed a few mail pieces using the information in this chapter, you will get a good feel for you cost per piece.

Before you try to decide on your direct mail reach, determine your annual direct mail budget. It is recommended that direct mail costs be the largest part of your advertising budget. Decide how many mailings you want to do in the year, at least six, and multiply your cost per piece by that number. That gives you your cost per recipient per year. Divide your budget by your cost per recipient and you will see how many names you can afford to mail to effectively.

$$\frac{\text{Total Budget}}{\text{Cost per Piece X Number of Mailings}} = \text{Number of Recipients}$$

Don't make the mistake of mailing to more names at the expense of frequency. Infrequent mailings to a large list are much less effective than frequent mailings to a smaller list.

The direct mail piece

Always remember the value of a consistent message. Although your mail pieces may have different objectives and design properties, they must still look like they came from the same source. Customers, no longer how long they have been with you, still need reassurance that you are solid and confident enough to maintain your identity.

Good direct mail pieces demand to be read! As an exercise in direct mail design, start paying careful attention to the mail you receive at home. Notice which pieces catch your eye and make you open the envelope, read the contents, and respond.

Conduct a little research and ask your spouse or another person in your household to save all mail after it's been read. Observe closely the pieces that were opened. What was it that made them read some pieces completely while leaving others unopened?

Here are some tips that will help get your direct mail pieces opened and read. Response depends largely on the offer, but if your envelope's not opened, you don't have a chance!

Quality

Everything you put in your prospects' and customers' hands should be printed on paper stock and by a printing process that's appropriate to the audience. The weekend-junket prospect may read an obviously mass produced cover letter, or one from a dot matrix printer, but the luxury-travel prospect should be addressed on classy paper stock with printing by a laser printer.

Highly effective newsletters can be created using inexpensive newsprint stock but these are directed at a bargain-basement market, not an upscale market. That doesn't mean you need a glossy magazine stock with four-color graphics for upscale promotions. But, your mail pieces should always reflect the level of sophistication of the product and the buyer. The prospect sees your mailings as an indicator of your level of sophistication.

The consistent use of color is important. Select an attractive color scheme that you will use for every printed piece that leaves your office. Even if you use just one color for economy, make it an attractive color that you use on everything, from business cards to brochures.

There are now sources for very attractive paper stock for use as brochures, letterhead, business cards and envelopes. Stock is available in a variety of colors and designs, and the right choice can give you a very professional look.

Have your printer quote a price for a custom-designed letterhead, envelope and business card. The printer or graphic artist can design a brochure shell to match. It's even possible to use different intensities (shades) of one color to give a two-color look at a one-color price.

A quick note about labeling: Do you open mail addressed to "resident"? Neither do your customers! Show some respect and address everyone by name. Any word processing program can create personalized labels from your database.

If you have a laser printer, use the clear laser labels rather than the tractor-fed white stickers. They look much more professional, and show that you are in business for real.

Newsletters

Your first contact with your customers may be with a newsletter. Your newsletter should be a simple, straight-forward design. It's meant to deliver evidence of your knowledge, and remind your customers that you are their supplier for whatever it is that you sell. It's not necessary to make it an artistic masterpiece, but it should be appropriate to the audience's level of sophistication.

If you don't have the time or talent to design and write your own newsletter, hire a professional. There are newsletter specialists advertised in your industry's trade press. Local print shops can recommend desktop publishers in your area as well. Local publishers will probably need more input from you, but may be more economical for small mailing lists.

Direct mail offers

Most direct mail pieces for specific offers will consist of the following components:

1. Envelope
2. Cover Letter
3. Promotional/Explanatory Material
4. Response Medium

The Envelope is, of course, the first thing the recipient sees. As you know from your experience as a recipient, the design of the envelope is what determines whether you will even see the other components.

Therefore, the envelope's objective is to get the recipient to look inside. You have to stir some degree of interest with the envelope. This can be done in a number of ways, but consider that a plain white number 10 business envelope with only your return address on the outside may not generate enough interest.

The best way to get an envelope opened is to offer a hint of what's inside. Envelope manufactures have come up with standard designs that have die-cut windows, zip-open doors, and pull-tabs to get the recipient involved in the piece immediately. If you intrique a customer into pulling tabs, or peeling off stickers, then the mailing produces a "lottery-ticket mentality." Make the envelope into a game that makes the prospect a participant rather than just a recipient.

Another way to get the reader curious is to use what mailers call a *dimensional piece*. A dimensional piece has a different shape than a plain envelope. Examples are mailing tubes, or small cartons. The postage you pay, and the cost of the package will go up considerably, but so will readership. Everyone is going to open a carton or tube!

A less expensive way to do a dimensional piece is to put something inside your envelope that the reader can feel when the envelope is held. One magazine publisher encloses a thin pencil in its renewal notices. The postal service limits the thickness of envelopes mailed at the one-ounce rate. Be sure to use the proper postage. Unsolicited mail arriving "postage due" will be refused and may alienate a customer or prospect.

Direct mail experts don't all agree on this, but when you're marketing on a shoestring, this writer strongly recommends that your name and identifying logo appear on everything you put into your prospects' hands. Even if they don't open the first envelopes you send, eventually they'll come to recognize you as a consistent mailer and may get curious enough to look inside.

The cover letter

Now that your prospect has opened the envelope, you have the opportunity to address him or her directly in your cover letter. There are entire books written on cover letter design and copy.

Here are a few tips that will help you get your message across.

Like the envelope, the letter must grab the reader's interest enough so that the whole letter is read.

Each letter should be addressed to the reader personally using your word processor's mail merge capability. Mail merge is the capability to personalize each letter with names you have selected from your database. Each will look like an individually prepared letter, with names, addresses and salutations customized.

Use the recipient's name again in the body of the letter. It catches the eye and compells him or her to read on. The recipient's name in the body of the letter should come at a key point. This sentence will definitely be read so make it count!

Before you sit down to write your letter, understand exactly what it is you are offering, and what it will do for the buyer.

Generally, your copy should appeal to one of these basic motivators:

Safety	Popularity	Exclusivity
Wealth/Economy	Style	Love
Comfort	Envy	Escape/Release
Self Esteem	Education	Discovery

Having determined what your offer is, think about which of these emotional hot-buttons it may push. For instance, if you are a travel agent working with a seniors' group tour, you can stress the security of traveling with an escorted group. Another benefit of the group tour is an opportunity to make new friends as well.

Which motivator would you use to promote a spa vacation? How about a singles trip?

You'll probably find more than one emotional appeal in any offer but emphasize just one or two in your advertising copy. Don't confuse the reader with too many emotional appeals. If you think of several, pick the one that you can make the best case for and drive it home.

Layout

Anything that is meant to be read should begin with a headline. The cover letter is no exception.

Once the envelope's been opened, your prospective customer must be pulled into the cover letter by a headline that gives a good reason to read on. The challenge of writing effective headlines is to grab the reader's attention with the implication of a benefit.

Recall the motivation you chose to pursue in the language of your direct mail piece. State it clearly in the headline with just a few words. For instance, if you are promoting a group cruise to a senior target market, you may choose "safety" as a motivator. Here is a short, clear headline:

Travel Safe and Secure

Following the headline is the usual personalized address and salutation.

The first paragraph is often the only one the reader will take time to read, so it's got to be strong. Describe the offer in terms of the emotional appeal you've chosen. This paragraph is devoted to benefit—what the product will do for the reader.

For your safety-conscious seniors, you might say:

Imagine, from your front door to the Caribbean and back, without a worry or care! Travel with an experienced escort from right here in Ourcity. Join our group of friends (and soon to be friends) on March 15, for our 7-day cruise.

Then, put in a few bulleted points to outline the actual included features of the offer (not too many—the accompanying brochure will give the full details). These should just be a few highlights to let the reader know what a treat you are offering!

Your cruise package includes:
- *All transportation, tips and taxes*
- *Baggage handling EVERYWHERE*
- *Six sumptuous meals each day*
- *Fully Escorted—Every Detail is Taken Care of!*

The next paragraph is where you use the reader's name to pull it all together. If you're promoting a group cruise for seniors, and using security as your appeal, you could say:

Mrs. Johnson, by traveling with our group you will know that I will be with you personally every step of the way. I watch out for every detail, so you can just relax and enjoy a worry-free vacation!

Then close with an appeal for some action;

Find out why people just like you travel with us year after year. You have to experience this level of attention to understand what it means to travel secure and coddled.

The letter is signed by you personally. Use a colored felt-tipped pen so it's clear that you signed it yourself.

Then, include a postscript that directs the reader to take some action:

PS: Call toll-free at 1–800–555–9999, or mail your reservation form in the enclosed postage paid envelope to reserve your space among friends.

Response media

Notice in that in the call to action, two different response media are provided: a toll-free phone number and a postage paid envelope.

If you want to increase the response to your direct mail, it's imperative that you make it easy, and free, for people to respond. If your mailing is to businesses, a fax order form will increase response, too. If they're ready to buy, you want to make it easy, and expedient to do so! Don't allow any reason to put your letter aside.

Watts telephone lines are now affordable, even for the home office. A business reply mail permit costs approximately $75 per year (check with your post office), plus the cost of envelopes and the actual postage. You only pay postage for envelopes that are mailed back to you.

A detailed brochure or product report should also be enclosed.

The cover letter is designed to get readers interested in as few words as possible. The detailed support material is there to answer their questions and give further important information.

If you don't have the time or inclination to design and execute your own direct mail program, help is available. Copywriters are available in any city and are listed in the Yellow Pages under Mailing Services. A good printer can also put you in touch with creative graphic designers, copywriters, and mailing services.

You can do as much or as little of the work as you want. Every step in the process can be hired out, including stuffing envelopes!

The keys to successful direct mail are the same as those for other media. Be consistent and repetitive, regarding both your message and price range. Speak consistently to your target customers, offering products and services that match their needs, desires and lifestyle. Keep the copy direct, focused on benefits, and end with a call to action and an easy way for the buyer to respond.

Direct mail takes patience. Since it takes six to seven exposures to make an impression, using direct mail will take time to work. But stick with it because direct mail is the only medium that guarantees the prospect will see your message. If you've mailed to someone six times in less than a year, and you've used my design tips, you are safe to assume that the prospective customer at least knows who you are.

The checklist on the following page will help you organize your mailing activities. If you have a staff, use their help. Doing direct mail programs all by yourself is a lot of work. Split up the duties like lining up co-op funds, designing mail pieces, stuffing and stamping.

Best of luck with your direct mail program!

Direct Mail Checklist

• PURPOSE
  • Maintain Contact • Specific Offer • Lead Generation
• PRODUCT
  Supplier _____ • Co-op proposal submitted by ___/___/___
  Product _____
  Are we sure this product is what our target customer wants to buy?
• LIST
  • Customers • Prospects • Outside List _____
  Number of pieces to be mailed _____
• BUDGET
  List Rental (if applicable) $ _____
  Design/Creative $ _____
  Printing/Paper stock $ _____
  Mailing Costs (Postage, Mail House) $ _____
• TIMING
  Selling season _____
  Mailing date _____

Objectives	Person Responsible	Initial
• Co-op funds approved ___/___/___	_____	_____
• Design/copy completed by ___/___/___	_____	_____
• Printing completed by ___/___/___	_____	_____
• Supporting material ready by ___/___/__	_____	_____
• Mailing prepared/stuffed by ___/___/___	_____	_____
• Delivered to Post Office ___/___/___	_____	_____

• MEASUREMENT

  _____ Responses Received by Mail
  _____ Responses Received by Phone
  _____ Sales consummated for total revenue of $ _____

• Report prepared/mailed for co-op funds, override commissions, bonus'.

Chapter 10

Print Media
Advertising

Many small businesses have a brief affair with print
media advertising, only to break up because tangible
results are not immediate. Entrepreneurs are
particularly impatient for results. After a few
advertisements, they expect the phone to begin
ringing off the hook. Print advertising takes time to
work, but it works.

Remember, it takes six or seven visual contacts with printed media before a prospective customer will recognize your name. You may have to run an advertisement 30 times in order for the same individual to see it those necessary six or seven times.

Advertising sales people will tell you that repetition is important. This is not a sales pitch—it's accurate information. If you run an advertisement once a week, it may well take 20 to 30 weeks before you see measurable results. Of course, the length of time before tangible results are produced is cut in half if you run two advertisements per week.

The question of frequency leads to the question of budget. If you are planning an advertising campaign in the newspaper, plan to run the advertisements weekly at the very least. If your budget won't bear at least 10 weekly advertisements, you cannot afford to advertise in a major metropolitan newspaper. There may, however, be a neighborhood or suburban paper that would work for you.

Naturally, your media selection will depend on what your target customer reads. By advertising in a suburban or neighborhood paper, you will target your advertising geographically. There's no need to pay for advertising that reaches hundreds of thousands of people, most of whom are unlikely to ever use your business. The 30,0000 people who subscribe to your local suburban paper are more likely prospects, and you won't be paying for the "overflow" coverage that advertising in the metropolitan paper creates.

Newspapers are not the limit

Many organizations publish their own newsletters. If your target customers belong to these organizations and clubs, then these newsletters offer a very targeted and affordable medium for small business advertising. Newsletters are usually monthly publications so it will take longer for your message to get through, but you'll find the overall cost of advertising very reasonable, which makes it a lot easier to be patient!

You can select organizations that, by their charter, have declared a common interest for their membership. There are clubs, associations, and organizations that draw their membership from very specific interest groups. Sports, arts, travel, religion, and hobbies are just a few of the special interests that draw people together into affinity groups.

If your products or services specifically match the needs of a local club or chapter of an affinity group, you should be a member of the group already. Obviously, you share their interests. Don't be shy about promoting yourself to fellow members of your organizations. Consumers prefer to do business with people they know and trust. However, you have to inform and emphasize that your business is designed to serve them specifically!

In addition to being impatient, entrepreneurs are usually very creative people as well. The problem with this combination of traits is that you are likely to get bored with the appearance of your advertisements, and will want to make creative changes regularly.

Resist the temptation to change your look! You may be sick and tired of your advertisements, but your prospective customer is not. In fact, the odds are that your prospective customer sees your print advertisement only once every three or four times it appears (this calculation assumes he or she reads regularly reads the publication). Your advertisements have to look the same every time, or the recognition does not accrue. Your image won't become familiar to prospective customers unless it looks the same every time it's seen.

Decide on a layout and typefaces that you are happy with and stick with the combination. You appear confident and solid by maintaining the same look. You appear indecisive and vague when you change your image from month to month. Imagine if you changed your personal appearance from week to week. Would people see you as confident and reliable? Would they recognize you easily?

The layout on the next page is an example of a simple, clean advertisement that can be used to promote any product or service.

HEADLINE

Ad copy - Ad copy - Ad copy

- *Bullets*
- *Bullets*   **$000.00**
- *Bullets*

Fine print - Fine print - Fine Print - Fine print

 GOURMET
Cruises and Tours
Address Phone Number
Office Hours

Take a look at the elements in this layout. The border is a simple, heavy black line. Ornate borders may attract the eye, but make sure the design is generally compatible with your products and services and doesn't impose a limit on future promotions. For instance, a travel agency may be tempted to use an anchor and chain motif. However, would these graphics be appropriate for a European tour promotion? Use a simple border that will be appropriate for any product or service your business offers now, or may add in the future. You don't want to have to make significant changes in the advertising layout to accommodate different offerings and promotions.

Select typefaces for your advertising copy (the printed words in the advertisement), carefully. Even though the copy in the advertisement will change for different products, you'll use the same typefaces to achieve a consistent image.

A rule of thumb is to use no more than two typefaces in the layout. Headlines should be in a bold, *sans serif* typeface. The characters in sans serif typefaces don't have little "feet" on them. The figure below shows the difference between serif and sans serif typefaces.

A a   A a

Serif Typeface   Sans Serif Typeface

The headline will be the largest print and use the fewest characters per line in the advertisement. Sans serif typefaces are well suited to headline applications.

Regarding the blocks of text, where the reader's attention is engaged for a whole sentence or more, those little "feet" on serif typefaces are helpful in easing the eye from word to word. The text of this book is printed in a serif typeface because it is easier for you to read.

Headlines

Now that you know you don't have to design new layouts all the time, you can use the time saved to write creative headlines. The headline of your advertisement should use as few words as possible. It is always in the same space in the layout, centered at the top.

When you read a newspaper, you decide which stories to read by their headlines. People automatically scan the pages until a headline grabs their attention. Your headline must compete with all the other headlines on the page, not just the other advertisements.

To get an idea of what a good headline looks and sounds like, start paying attention to which ones grab you. Don't just look at other advertisements. Note the effective headlines of stories as well and begin to maintain an "idea file." Clip catchy advertisements and story headlines and use them for inspiration when you're trying to write a good advertisement of your own.

A good headline gives readers a taste of the story (or product), and compels them to read on. A common mistake in print advertising by small businesses is the use of the company name as a headline. Your company name doesn't give people a reason to stop and read your advertisement. It belongs at the bottom of the advertisement (see the sample advertising layout).

Try to state a benefit in the headline. The difference between benefits and features is that features are components of the product while benefits are what things the product does for the buyer.

The bullet points in the advertisement should also highlight benefits. To appeal to readers, you must indicate "what's in it for them." Their motivation to buy will most likely be based on their application of the pleasure principle, not their appreciation of your product's nuts and bolts. By the way, limit the number of benefits to two or three. Don't get carried away in your advertising copy, making the offer sound unbelievable.

Always talk directly to your target audience, in language they understand. The benefits you identify and the language you use should be appealing to your audience. Be sure you're tuned into your reader's point of view, not just your own.

Marketing experts are not all in agreement on the next practice. This writer recommends that a product advertisement state a price. The sample layout features the price as a major component of the advertisement because, with this information, consumers can know whether or not you speak the same language.

To talk to your target customers and leave an impression, you must tell them that your products are in their price range. When you see an advertisement for an automobile, doesn't the price largely determine whether you read the rest of the copy? Your customers have a price range in their minds and shop for most of the things they buy with that as a reference.

By stating a price, you identify yourself with a specific group. Also, by including prices in your advertisements, you are committing your business to continuity in pricing. To talk to the same customers consistently, you must be in their price range consistently.

There is very little copy called for in the sample ad. Make your points in as few words as possible, then direct the reader to take action.

The last line of the advertisement should be a call to action. "Don't miss this opportunity, call today!" gives the reader a sense of urgency. Readers must be motivated to act before they turn the next page. A strategy many advertisements use is to provide a coupon that compels the reader to clip and save the advertisement.

Response media

Response media are communicative techniques that inspire your prospective customer to respond to you. A coupon is one way to provide the reader with an easy and memorable way to respond to your advertisement.

That's why your company name, logo, telephone number and hours are placed at the bottom of the advertisement. The last thing read (everyone reads top to bottom) should be easy to remember and should encourage a response.

Your logo becomes an icon. Like those simple, little pictures on the computer screen that represent complicated programs, your company's logo is a visual cue that helps your customers remember your business. A logo is much easier to remember than a name; this is why it's so important to have a simple, descriptive logo at the bottom of your advertisement.

Your logo should uniquely identify and describe your business. The logo in the sample advertisement does both very simply and clearly.

The address is there to tell customers *where* to go and the hours tell them *when* they can stop in or call.

Clever telephone numbers that spell easy-to-remember words are excellent response media. It may cost extra to obtain a specific phone number. But if your customers will be doing business with you by phone, an easy-to-remember number will be a real convenience for them. They don't have to save the advertisement or look you up in the Yellow Pages (where they'll see your competitors' advertisements) to find you.

You may become bored with this layout, but not your customers. They don't see it every day like you do. Resist the creative temptation to change your advertisement repeatedly.

A consistent, repetitive message and layout will reap big dividends in the long run.

Chapter 11

Multimedia Promotions

If you're on a shoestring budget, you may have assumed it was impossible to create an effective multimedia promotion. The truth is, multimedia approaches are an excellent and economical way to make a number of impressions on your audience in a compressed amount of time.

Multimedia simply means projecting the same message in more than one media. Electronic media may or may not be involved.

Your newspaper advertisement layout (Chapter 10 describes advertising layouts in detail) provides an excellent foundation for a multimedia promotion.

Once you have created your standard layout, you will change only the copy to reflect the product or service you are promoting with each campaign. The multimedia campaign will take one product advertisement and use it in a number of different formats. The objective is to present your target audience with one message (based on that advertisement) in several modes.

The pieces will be in different sizes and shapes, so you may need a little help from a graphic artist to establish the proportional dimensions of the advertisement in its variations. But like the newspaper advertisement layout, you'll only have to hire the graphic artist for your first multimedia project. Have the different shapes created without product information so you have blank templates for future multimedia campaigns.

To carry out this campaign, you must do some planning. Your game plan should account for the fact that it takes six or seven contacts for a consumer to "get the message." All forms of effective advertising require frequency and repetitions. The advantage of multimedia promotions is that you can hit the consumer with six or seven impressions in a very short period of time, say a week or two. It's a great way to promote a product that will be available for a short period of time. For instance, a travel agency might effectively use a multimedia program to promote a short term air fare sale. Since the sale is only for a limited period, there isn't time to convey your message to the consumer by a series of newspaper advertisements alone.

Depending on your business, and your target audience, you can choose from a virtually unlimited list of media options. Let's use the example of the travel agency promoting a fare sale.

The advertisement layout might promote travel to a few specific cities and include sample prices. (In this writer's opinion, the consumer wants pricing information from advertisements. Advertisements that say "Save 40%!" are too vague. Real numbers such as "Chicago to Los Angeles $149" are much more useful.) Here's just a partial list of the many media you could use to place this same advertisement in front of your target customer several times in a short period:

Go to a quick sign shop and have the advertisement enlarged to banner size and poster size. Display the banner outside your business and paste posters back to back and hang them from your ceiling inside.

On a copy machine, you can enlarge the advertisement to 8" x 11" for use as a flyer, mailer, newspaper or newsletter insert, and counter card. Put it under windshield wipers in your parking lot, enclose a copy in your mailing to your customer and prospect lists, enclose a copy with each invoice, fax copies, hand out copies on the street corner!

Print the same advertisement as a post card for an inexpensive mailer.

To add impact, use brightly colored paper. Don't forget to be consistent. Use the same color on each of the different media you use.

Use your imagination! The multimedia promotion is a great way to get multiple exposures in a short period of time.

Chapter 12

Show Exhibits

Ask five people who have worked trade or consumer shows and you'll get five different opinions on their value. The reason you'll hear mixed results is that most people don't do the homework that's necessary to be successful at shows.

There are two ways to work a show. The first way is as an attendee networking with the businesses that have rented booths. The second way to work a show is as an exhibitor, renting a booth from which you display and sell your product or service.

Attending shows is, of course, the less expensive route. As an attendee, you'll be trying to make as many face-to-face contacts as possible. Remember, however, that the businesses that rented booths are there to *sell*. If they are at the right show, and doing their jobs properly, exhibitors won't have time to talk to anyone but qualified prospects for their products.

In fact, you must be careful not to be an intruder. They've paid dearly for their booth space and have to limit themselves to activities that will provide a return on that investment.

Booth rental can be expensive, which means you have to choose very carefully which shows you'll participate in as an exhibitor.

Which shows?

When deciding in which shows to exhibit, remember that all important question: "Who will I be talking to?" Most businesses that get poor results at shows are exhibiting at inappropriate shows. To get your best results, determine your "reach" and compare it with the reach of the show. Some shows attract a national audience, some a local audience. Don't spend the money to exhibit at national shows unless your organization is equipped to follow up and service business at the national level.

There are basically two different kinds of shows:

- Business to business shows
- Consumer shows

There are literally thousands of shows of both types, around the world, throughout the year.

Business to business shows are, as the title implies, opportunities to display your product or service to an audience of buyers who represent other businesses.

Many business to business shows are specific to one industry. Those are referred to as *trade shows* since all exhibitors and attendees have an interest in the same trade. If your product or service is designed to serve the needs of organizations in a specific industry, trade shows are the place for you.

For instance, if you've come up with a product that streamlines some manufacturing process, you would look for trade shows that attract the decision makers in manufacturing. If your product is designed for a specific industry, your selection of shows will be straightforward. You will look for shows that attract buyers from the manufacturing managers in that industry.

Many associations sponsor trade shows for their members. You may have to be an affiliate member of the association to exhibit at some association shows. If the members of the association are all good prospects for your product or service, you may want to consider joining anyway.

As with any effective marketing activity, you want to narrow the field of people to whom you promote. You want to exhibit at shows that draw the highest possible percentage of real prospects for your product or service.

Consumer shows are typically focused on a certain type of buyer. For instance, a sports and vacation show would attract mostly "outdoors" types. A "home and garden" show would attract only homeowners who are considering some sort of remodeling or redecorating.

There are consumer shows that appeal to many different kinds of buyers. Take the time to find the ones that attract your target customer group.

Many shows are seasonal. For instance, home and garden shows are held in the early spring to catch buyers thinking about summer projects. Skiing shows are held in the early fall to generate interest for the coming season.

Seasonal shows are a great way to kick off the selling season if yours is a seasonal industry. They are timed to put you in front of buyers in the early stages of their buying process.

Generally, show promoters clearly identify their target audience. The work has already been done for you! All you have to do is select the shows that attract the audience you want to talk to. For more information on trade shows, contact the International Exhibitors Association at (703) 941–3725.

The action plan

A large group of buyers, almost all of whom are likely prospects for your product or service, is likely to be your idea of a dream-come-true. The reality of this dream is that, while you'll be surrounded by prospects, you'll also be surrounded by your most formidable competitors.

If you are going to come away from this show with lots of new business, you have to plan carefully.

Step one is to identify clearly your objectives at this show.

Why are you here? Are you solidifying your market position with an audience that already knows you, or are you trying to expand into a new market?

What is your market position in this room of exhibitors? Are you a leader among the other vendors exhibiting at this show? Are you the challenger in a new market? As with your other promotional media, everything must reflect your market position. Your display, handout materials, signs, attitude, and language should all reflect your market position.

Don't depend on luck or location to draw a crowd at your booth.

Smart exhibitors start contacting their prime prospects well before the actual show date. If you can obtain a list of people who have registered as attendees, you can do an advance mailing that invites them to your booth.

You may have a drawing for a door prize to entice them. Mail the registration form in advance so they'll come to the show looking for you.

Another enticement is a discount for purchases made on the day of the show. An advance mailing could inform prospects of the specials you'll be offering. Prepare your prospects to come to the show both looking for you and ready to buy!

Your display

When designing your display, remember that you are projecting your business' image. You want to project an image that will get people's attention, make you recognizable, and display your product or service attractively.

Register early for shows so you have the most options in selecting the location of your booth. Look at the floor plan to anticipate the natural traffic pattern at the show (when you attend a show, you tend to walk the aisles in a certain order). Most people automatically turn right when they walk in the main entrance. Try to be on that side of the room, close to the entrance. Corner booths are visible from a greater distance, and from more directions. You may pay extra for a corner, but it's worth it if your display is well designed.

You want to be identifiable from at least 25 feet away. That means posters, signs and graphic designs should be clearly discernible from that distance.

Have a good sign professionally printed. The white card provided by the trade show promoter is not enough! Sign shops can help create a sign that utilizes your colors, logo and message. To attract even more attention, use a banner that spans most of the width of your booth.

Don't clog your signs with text. To attract qualified prospects, display just enough information to identify who you are and what you are offering.

Your aim is visual impact so to as many shows as you can to see what works. Incorporate the best ideas into your own business.

Observe which booths draw a crowd. What attracts people? The best booths stand out from the others in some way. That doesn't necessarily mean you have to invest in a large, professionally designed display. Free popcorn, popped on the spot so the aroma filled the room, has been used as an extremely effective trade-show bait. Be careful, though. Giving away popcorn may make you popular, but it doesn't close sales or filter out the nonprospects (those who roam trade show floors, methodically picking up all the freebies they can carry out the door).

The purpose of the display is to draw prospects to you. The people working in your booth must then make face-to-face, one-on-one contact with prospective customers. This direct contact is vital; never make handout materials available for people to pick up and walk away with without talking to you first. Remember, you attend shows to make contact with prospects. If they aren't interested enough to at least talk to you about your product or service, they're not real prospects.

The handout material

The direct mail chapter of this book offers ideas on designing direct mail pieces for impact. The same ideas apply to the handout materials you bring to the show.

Premium products justify premium collateral materials. If you're selling a "top shelf" product, everything about your display should be "top shelf," as well as the materials the prospect takes home.

Each prospect will be taking home your materials, and those from your competitors at the show. During that face-to-face, one-on-one contact, you should do something that personalizes your material for the prospect.

During your conversation, make notes that apply specifically to the project or purchase your prospective customer is considering. Drawings, price estimates or useful advice in your pen will help your prospective customer recall the contact.

The contact

The conversation with your prospective customer at the show is your opportunity to demonstrate your expertise and personal support of your product or service.

Beautiful displays featuring excellent collateral materials become ineffective facades when staffed by temporaries who know virtually nothing about the product. The people who work your booth have to be your top sales people.

Since you'll be spending significant amounts of money to participate in a show, it makes sense to send the people who can best take advantage of the exposure on the front line. Their appearance and attitude can make or break your show experience. Dress is governed by the type of show you're working. What is appropriate at a sports and vacation show may not be appropriate at a computer and technology show. Common sense should guide you and you may have to guide your people.

Many shows last several days and require many hours standing and talking with prospective customers. These conditions are tough on unmotivated employees. Working a trade show booth, and making it lucrative, takes endurance and desire. Make sure your sales people are rewarded well for sales resulting from your trade show participation.

Follow-up

It doesn't take long for people to forget who they talked to at a show. After all, they talked to you and all of your competitors in one afternoon! Therefore, for follow-up to be effective, it has to begin immediately.

One method to obtain basic information on your prospects is to have all the people who visit your booth fill out an entry form for a door prize. Your sales people can write notes on the back of the entry form regarding the project or product discussed.

Even if they don't buy from you this time, you should have identified some good prospects for future business. You'll want to add these names and addresses to your prospect mailing list, too. People who won't give you their addresses are probably not real prospects. Since you can't deliver a door prize without an address, toss the entries that aren't complete.

An old saying by successful sales people go like this: "Follow up until the prospect either buys or dies." This book recommends that you also practice a variation on that adage. People visited your booth because your company, your product and the people that present your information impressed them. You spent a lot of money and time to make contact with them. Therefore, you ought to, "Keep prospects alive until they buy!"

Analyze results

After each show is over, and prospects have been followed up, analyze the results you got from that show. Most shows are annual events and you want to know if your return on investment warrants renting a booth at next year's show. Ask yourself and your employees,

"What was this particular show was good for?" Note what types of prospects and competitors were there. Did a lot of current customers show up or were they all new prospects?

Start thinking about next year's objective.

You may conclude that this show would be a good place to roll out a new product next year. It may be the place to reinforce your market position with current customers. Or, it may have been a waste of money. In this case, you know to spend the money elsewhere next year!

Chapter 13

Promotional Events

Perhaps you've attended lively events promoting other businesses and thought to yourself, "I wish I could draw a crowd like this."

With a little ingenuity and imagination, you can stage events that generate excitement for your company and your products or services. Drawing a crowd doesn't have to cost a lot of money.

First, have a clear vision of what you are trying to accomplish with a promotional event. Of course, your objective is to sell more of your product or service, but be even more specific about your tactics. For example, some events are designed to penetrate your current market more extensively while others are intended to reach new prospects.

As with every other decision you make, the most important consideration is your target customer. The event must be designed to attract and appeal to people who fit your target customer profile.

There are basically two ways to get involved in promotional events: you can plan your own or you can rent space from or cosponsor-sponsor events that are already planned, often by professional promoters.

The latter may be a good way to get started if you're not comfortable with the risk and expense involved in planning an event from scratch.

In Des Moines, there is an annual Grand Prix race that takes place on our downtown streets. For four days, the streets are closed to traffic and converted to a track. The event draws thousands of people and generates interest in automotive cosmetics, performance, and safety.

The audience is a highly qualified group for any business that deals in automotive service, parts, accessories, apparel and related items.

This is a large scale event that offers exposure to a fairly specific type of customer draws from a broad geographic area. There are many events like this around the country that you can get involved in at relatively little expense.

Think about the major events that are staged in your community and identify the ones that draw your target audience. Unless a large percentage of the people in attendance fit your target customer profile, you'll be wasting money on "overflow."

Also keep in mind that the bulk of the audience at these events will be people who have never heard of you before. Large public events are good for exposure to new prospective customers but are unlikely to reach many of your current customers unless you specifically invite them.

The strategy for big events

The strategy here, then, is to develop new leads from prospects you may never meet elsewhere. This kind of promotion is ideal for a growth stage that calls for reaching new markets. See Chapter 17 for a more thorough discussion of growth strategies. If you are not pursuing one of the strategies that seeks new markets, then these events are not appropriate for you.

By drawing prospective customers to your display, as you would at a trade or consumer show, you create the opportunity to capture as much information about the prospective customers as you can.

Registration for a door prize is an easy way to get this information. The door prize doesn't have to be a car, but it does have to be significant enough to make people take the time to register.

Ask for some demographic information on the registration cards and throw away the ones that aren't complete. If people aren't willing to answer a few questions, don't consider them prospective customers—they're only interested in the prize!

Then design some way of following up, at least by mail, within a week of the event. Don't give prospective customers time to forget you before you make the first follow-up contact.

The suggestions for working from trade show exhibit booths (Chapter 12) applies here as well. The important points are to capture database information and to follow up immediately thereafter.

Your own events

Planning your own events will take more effort and money on your part, but you can attract only the people you want with no overflow.

Just because it's your own event doesn't mean you have to go it totally alone. Suppliers, noncompetitive merchants who want access to the same people, and other strategic alliances (see Chapter 18), may want to get involved. Their participation will make your event bigger, possibly draw new prospects from others' mailing lists, and save money. By involving other organizations, you can probably multiply the number of prizes available, giving people even more incentive to attend.

Here are some of the items you'll have to plan and budget for when staging your own events:

Meeting Space—The location of your promotion reflects your business' image. Although space in the most elegant hotel in town is expensive, if you are selling a premium product to upscale customers, it's appropriate for the promotion. Of course, the reverse is true for a bargain-basement product promotion staged for the economy-minded shopper. If your promotion is a garage sale, hold it in a garage!

Prizes—Nothing draws traffic like good door prizes. Drawings also provide a response medium of sorts as the prize registration form collects whatever information you want to ask. These forms also serve as tracking devices for leads generated by the promotional event, allowing you to assess the promotion's general results.

Entertainment—This can mean live music, a recital by a local dance studio, a demonstration, video, or lecture relevant to your product or its use...whatever will appeal to your target audience and support the promotion. If you want them to stick around, entertain them.

Refreshments—Peanuts and soda are appropriate for some audiences, champagne and hors d'oeuvres for others. Foods prepared on the spot, like popcorn or cotton candy, also serve as entertainment. If possible, relate the choice of refreshments to the product and make sure they appeal to the target audience.

One the other hand, don't overspend on entertainment and refreshments. An excess of either won't close more sales, it will just cost you more.

Staffing—Your sales people should all make themselves available for the duration of your event and be given incentives for sales that can be tracked directly to the promotional event.

Clerical and administrative staff can be used for greeting, registration and serving refreshments.

Staffing may be your biggest expense but your people are critical to taking full advantage of the opportunities afforded by the promotional event.

Whether you stage a promotional event yourself or participate in an event organized by another, be prepared to "do it up." If you're reluctant for any reason, you're better off not doing it at all or waiting until you are prepared and energized.

Chapter 14

Public Relations

A recent national survey found that more than 90 percent of readers believe what they read in newspaper or magazine articles. Compare that to the only 8 percent of people who believe what they read in advertisements. It seems, then, that a news story reporting on you and/or your business might leave a significant impression on the reader's mind.

But how do you get good "ink" from your local newspaper and magazine publishers?

Many business owners use an ineffective approach to getting coverage in their local newspapers or magazines. Perhaps you've sent press releases with no results. After a couple of tries, you concluded it was hopeless and gave up.

Here are some tips to increase your chances of receiving coverage. Before you approach any publication's editor, take some time to identify which publications are worthy of the effort. Again, refer to your target customers. What publications do they read? What kinds of stories will pique their interest? As with advertising, you want to address your target customers directly by using media they are likely to subscribe to or read regularly.

Such relevant publications may be your local newspaper or the state-wide business magazine. There may be a local TV or radio talk show that appeals to the same people you're after.

Find out what your customers pay attention to and concentrate your efforts only on those media or programs.

You also have to develop links with media that cover stories about your industry. You have to fit into their programming in order to have any chance of making an appearance.

PR also means press relations

If you keep in mind that the media's responsibility to the public is to report newsworthy information, you will be on the right track. Reporters and editors are looking for accurate, timely information that will be of interest to the reader. So, if your press releases sound like advertising copy rather than newsworthy information, they will be ignored.

Writing good releases is only part of the process. Before you have any chance of finding your story on the business page, you have to establish a relationship with someone at the publication.

One of the best ways to get the media's attention is to establish yourself as an industry insider or expert. If you are active in your national and regional trade associations (and it is highly recommended that you be very active!), you will often be abreast of important news stories before the press has access to them.

If you can regularly offer "scoops" that are of interest to local readers to the publication you're targeting, your reporter contact will call you first when the publication wants to quote an industry source.

Get to know business section reporters and feed them stories whenever you can in order to establish yourself as that publication's "industry expert."

Take it a step further and you may be able to write a regular column for your local newspaper or business-oriented magazine. If you have writing talent and can discipline yourself to produce a newsworthy column on a regular basis, this enterprise may be for you.

Before you contact your intended editor, write three or four good stories to provide as sample pieces to submit along with your proposal (these stories also become backup pieces should the need arise).

If your local newspaper or business magazine is not interested, propose your idea to the editor of your chamber of commerce newsletter or area associations that have an interest in your industry. After your material has appeared regularly in one publication, you have a track record to show to larger publications.

Articles or stories in publications specific to your trade don't just develop your reputation among your peers, they give you credibility as an industry expert in general. Reprints of trade press stories can be mailed to your customers and prospects. They are also supporting material for proposals to your local newspaper or other media.

Broadcast media

The process is the same with broadcast media. The difference is, instead of writing, you are going to have to be prepared to speak, often extemporaneously. If you're to be interviewed, you must be articulate and able to present facts in language the listening public will understand. Broadcast news reporters are looking for the same newsworthy information that print media reporters are. The difference is, they want it live and now.

Those of you who are comfortable speaking may want to get yourself booked as a guest on that talk show that's popular among your customers. You'll establish a high profile in your community, while establishing yourself as the expert the station can call when it needs a quote.

Just as newspapers may be receptive to a regular column, broadcast media may be as well.

A local television station in Des Moines broadcasts a weekly feature on gardening and landscaping during its weather segments on the morning, evening, and late night news programs.

A local landscaper gives seasonal information about planting, fertilizing lawns, preparing plants for winter, whatever is timely. The station credits him and his business at the beginning and end of each segment and he wears a green blazer which sports his company name and logo. He's a local celebrity and recognized as an expert in his field (no pun intended). The station gives viewers useful, timely and accurate information. The landscaper does all the work and research and appears as a credible news source. It's a classic *win-win* relationship: both parties, the station and the landscaper, are better off as a result of their collaboration.

If you don't know if you can present yourself well in person, don't present yourself at all. Negative exposure in the media is worse than no exposure. If you don't feel confident that you can portray yourself as an expert, you're better off employing a different media or studying the guidelines for public speaking presented in Chapter 8.

Contacting the press

Letters to the editor and editorials are ways to introduce yourself as a credible source. The first time you make a media contact, start with a cover letter that cites your credentials, describes how long you've been in business, notes the associations you are active in, and highlights the business experience that qualifies you to comment. Include a reprint of an article you wrote, or that was written about you, as additional qualification. Your editorial comment is much more likely to gain attention if the editor knows a little bit about your background before he or she begins reading. If you want to propose a regular column or talk show appearance, this procedure is a good way to get your foot in the door.

Follow-up

After allowing time for your press release (or other materials) to arrive and for the editor to read it, a follow-up call is in order. Don't wait any longer than a week to follow up. You're letter may be forgotten by then!

Simply call to introduce yourself and ask if the editor has questions or needs more information. Offer yourself as a source who can add interest and depth to the publication or program.

If this editor isn't interested in your story, ask if he or she knows of another editor or station manager who may be. Then contact the "editor B" by saying you were referred by "editor A."

The press release

Like good advertising, a good press release starts with a headline of sorts. The first line of your release should be a statement that gives the reader an idea of the content to come and why it deserves reading. What makes this story important to the reader? For instance, if you're reporting the results of a survey, start with a synopsis of the results:

"Industry survey finds 32% of homes have faulty wiring."

In the body of the release, get immediately down to business. Keep it simple, brief, and to the point.

Tell the reader who conducted the survey, and why the results are important. The reader will want to know how to find out if his or her home is one of the dangerous ones and how to get the problem corrected (which probably requires contacting you!).

Offer a "free home inspection to the readers of ABC Tribune" and tell them how to get in touch with you. This release does three things: it releases important news of a problem most people were not aware of, gives an exclusive benefit to the readers of the ABC Tribune, and presents you as the one who can solve the problem.

Being quotable

Whether you are writing an editorial, or responding to a call from the press, you want to give memorable information that the media can use. The most successful politicians speak in "sound bites." The reader or listener then associates them with those brief statements. "I have a dream," and "Ask not what your country can do for you..." are examples of memorable quotes. Both were used to make strong points easy for the listener to remember.

Never exaggerate or make up details to spice up a story. Reporters and editors have a responsibility to report the truth. They want to know that they can trust you for accuracy. If you don't know the answer, or can't name the source you're quoting, practice the rule, "If in doubt, leave it out!"

Being a good neighbor

Public relations is not a one-time promotion or stunt. Your company should do everything possible to be a good neighbor by participating in community activities, charities and benevolent organizations. It's also a good idea to encourage your employees to be active in the community. You can do that be offering paid time off to volunteer for qualifying activities.

Write clear rules delineating the scope of your offer so there can be no misunderstandings. You don't want participation in outside activities to bring you negative public relations so make sure you're supporting noncontroversial organizations and causes.

In Chapter 13, you will find some ideas on special events that you can sponsor that will do something nice for your community, while giving your business excellent exposure.

Your community nourishes the customers who support your business, the employees who work for you, and the environment in which you operate. Give as much as you can magnanimously. It will come back to you!

Chapter 15

Guarantees

Probably the largest single factor in a prospective customer's decision regarding whether or not to do business with you for the first time is the degree of risk he or she perceives there to be in the transaction.

By stating a guarantee, you can reduce or eliminate the risk on behalf of your buyer. In fact, guarantees shift the risk from the buyer to the seller.

Trust is another significant factor in the customer's decision to purchase goods or services from you. When you offer a product or service in exchange for the customer's money, you also offer the pledge that your product or service will perform as intended. The customer must trust that you will keep your promise (you, on the other hand, can be much more confident about the performance of the customer's money!).

The guarantee tells your current and prospective customers that they can trust you, that they can believe what you say, and that they are not really taking a chance at all by doing business with you.

Unconditional guarantees

The unconditional guarantee says that, "No matter why you're dissatisfied, tell us and we'll refund your money. No questions asked."

The unconditional guarantee virtually eliminates risk for the customer. If, after returning home and taking a second look at the product, your customer concludes that the color is wrong and that purchasing it was a bad decision after all, it can be returned with no questions asked.

Conditional guarantees

If you are uncomfortable with the idea of "no questions asked," you may place limits on the scope of your guarantee. You can specify the conditions under which restitution will be made and in what form.

The conditions may demand that the customer assemble, maintain, or use the product according to directions. The conditions may specify what results the customer can expect and/or when results will become evident.

For example, an exterminator may promise that customers will not be troubled by insects in their homes, provided they purchase monthly applications. If insects are detected, the exterminator will return to the residence and spray again without charge.

You may limit the life of the guarantee, or require that the product be returned in good condition.

Automotive warranties specify a limited length of time and/or mileage. They also limit their guarantee to specific parts. Some warrantied repairs include the cost of installing the replacement parts while others do not.

The more conditions you place on the guarantee, the more risk you shift back to the customer. A guarantee that is too limited or complex may confuse or overwhelm the customer. Ironically, you risk driving the customer away with an overly limited guarantee.

Buyer's remorse

Have you ever bought something and then immediately began wondering whether or not it was such a good idea? Most of us have, and the larger the dollar amount spent, the more we question our own wisdom. This is called buyer's remorse. The guarantee also reassures the buyer that he or she will not experience that uncomfortable syndrome.

The more expensive an item is, the more reassurance the customer will need. Would you buy a new car without a significant warranty?

Automobile manufacturers add value to their cars by including longer or less limited warranties in the purchase price. Many higher priced cars automatically carry an extended or more liberal warranty to counteract a bad case of buyer's remorse.

When constructing your own guarantee, consider first the nature of your product. Since customer's expectations vary widely (one customer buys a car for prestige, another buys the same car for reliable transportation), the guarantee must specify how the customer can reasonably expect the product or service to perform, and what you will do if it does not.

The *unconditional guarantee* returns virtually all of the risk in the transaction to the seller. The *conditional guarantee* limits exposure for both parties by sharing the risk.

The trust factor is also a component in the transaction. The more you limit your promise, the less you engender trust.

The promises you make in the selling process will be construed as a guarantee. A written guarantee will clarify customer expectations and protect both of you in the long run.

Chapter 16

Samples

The sample, like the guarantee, is a powerful risk-reducing agent. By giving the customer a chance to try or experience your product or service before actually buying it, you help diminish any element of risk he or she may be sensing.

There are several different ways to offer samples and your approach will depend on the product or service you offer.

One of the tactics used when launching my speaking career was to offer free presentations to audiences that included potential customers. By speaking at the national convention of the American Society of Association Executives (professionals who book speakers for their own association meetings), prospective customers were given "free samples." This way, association executives could make booking decisions based on their own experience—they would know what they were buying.

If you offer a service that prospective clients can experience for a limited time without obligation, you could give them a chance to try your service without risk. For example, assume you're an accountant serving small businesses and you offer two months of limited service free so they can experience what it's like to have books and income statements prepared on time and have someone else deal with what they consider to be a headache.

You've got a chance to prove your value, and hopefully, get them "hooked" on the service. Will everyone buy? No. Will this take up some of your time? Yes. But if you're not as busy as you'd like to be, then you can afford to invest a little time. It's at least as valuable as time spent making cold calls.

As with a guarantee, you are assuming the risk for the customer.

Software vendors sometimes entice users by providing free or inexpensive sample versions. The sample version may not have all of the capabilities or capacity of the full system. Or it may only run for a limited amount of time and then deny access so you either have to buy the system or return to your old ways.

An important caveat is to make sure the customer knows how to use the sample. If a prospective customer becomes frustrated with the sample version, it's not likely that he or she will buy the product.

Some products are inexpensive enough so that full-function sample can be virtually given away. This strategy is only appropriate if it is a product people will have to replace.

For instance, you've received toothpaste samples in the mail or with your Sunday newspaper. People grow up using the toothpaste their parents use and don't change brands easily. When was the last time you bought a different brand of toothpaste just for the sake of trying something new?

New breakfast cereals are marketed the same way. You probably buy the same one or two breakfast cereals over and over. You don't go to the cereal section and look for new brands to try every time you go to the grocery store.

But you might try a free sample.... If it's good enough and gives you a compelling reason to change brands, you'll do it. But if you hadn't received the free sample, you probably never would have given the new product a chance.

You may want to offer the sample in exchange for some commitment from the customer. You may exchange the sample for something the customer has to offer you, a sort of barter. If you do barter a sample, make sure the terms of future exchanges are understood.

In terms of your product or service, determine how a customer can try your product without risk and then become compelled to purchase the full-function version.

The strategy you'll use depends on how much you have invested in the product sample and how much of a sample the prospective customer will have to sample before becoming hooked.

Chapter 17

Growth Strategy

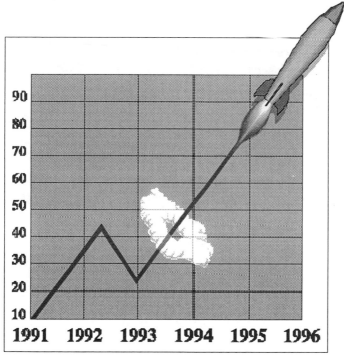

No matter how successful your business is today, you should always be planning for your business' future success. The refrain, "If you're not growing, you're dying," is relevant to this chapter.

An effective growth strategy focuses on two dimensions: products and customers. Very simply, there are only three real growth strategies possible:

New Products to Current Customers

Current Products to New Customers

New Products to New Customers

A fourth strategy will be identified later, but you will see that it is based on one of the three listed here.

No matter how long you have been in business, you have undoubtedly found a comfort level with either a particular product or type of customer.

The money budgeted for expansion is always above and beyond current budgets for the same activity. You don't want to dilute your efforts to retain your current customers and to convert the prospects you've already started cultivating. This new activity, expansion, calls for new money.

The first strategy focuses on your *current customers*, people who already do business with you. They are comfortable with you, and you have already come up with some solutions to their needs.

This trust factor automatically gives you a foot in the door for sales of new products to current customers.

New products to current customers

This approach carries the least amount of risk of the three expansion strategies. Most of the new money you will budget for this strategy is in the area of *product development* (see Chapter 3). You already have the customer; the next step is to develop, or add, products that satisfy needs not satisfied by your current products.

If your business resells products provided by wholesalers or contracted manufacturers, there is very little cost to this strategy. Instead, you will focus very carefully on the process of *product selection*.

The key risk involved is the possibility of eroding the trust you have established in the past by introducing products that do not serve the customer well. Good market research will minimize the risk.

Market research for new product development or selection can be conducted with the help of the actual end user. One way of doing this is through *customer focus groups*. To conduct a customer focus group, invite a number of your customers, hopefully a representative cross section of the people who do business with you, to give input on the new product idea.

How you get their input is up to you: written surveys, face-to-face meetings, and telephone conversations are all productive methods.

This writer serves on what one industry magazine calls an "Editorial Advisory Board," which functions as a sort of customer focus group. We were selected as a group because we are typical of the magazine's readers. We meet about once each year to discuss editorial content, design changes, and general thrust of the magazine. In exchange, the publisher pays travel, lodging and dinner expenses and our names are listed inside the front cover of the magazine. If your customers, or at least the ones in your focus group, are all local, you can run ideas past them for the cost of a lunch or dinner. (It's nice if there's a little benefit for the members of the focus group, too. A little recognition is enough for most people. Seeing my name in that magazine every month is a definite boost for me!)

Customer focus groups can validate your new product idea, predict the acceptance by the general buying public and even help you refine the new product design. A new product that is blessed by a customer focus group is practically guaranteed acceptance.

To best take advantage of your past success, new products should be related to your original products, or natural extensions of the original product line.

Don't add products that compete with a line you already carry. The new product should be a natural extension of your current line, enabling you to capture new sales without eroding existing sales. In other words, you want to capture sales that would have occurred somewhere else if you hadn't added the new product.

For example, if you operate a successful travel agency and want to expand your product line, there are numerous possibilities. Your clients are loyal and book all of their travel arrangements through you. Since they already rely on you for their travel arrangements, you want to offer a new product line that will compliment the business, without shifting market share from one current supplier to another.

What else do people who travel buy? They may need luggage or other travel accessories. Where do they have their film developed after a trip? If your clients regularly buy sunspot getaways in the winter, could you sell them a pre-trip tan with a tanning bed? A bookstore section could feature travel guides, maps, and videos to help with trip preparation. They probably go to a bookstore to buy those now. Why not capture those sales in house?

New product development calls for imagination. Brainstorming sessions with everyone in your business may bring up ideas you wouldn't think of on your own. Those client focus groups may come right out and tell you what else they would be interested in buying from you!

If you have a product that is bringing your current customers back time and time again, you may want to examine the second strategy, that of selling current products to new customers.

Current products to new customers

You are expanding your *reach* with this strategy. You already know that expanding your reach to contact new prospects will require a considerable increase in your advertising and promotion budget. No product development cost is incurred with this strategy, so the only budget risk will be money spent promoting to new markets.

When looking at new markets, you are either looking for a different geographic group or a different demographic group. Before you try to expand either one, be sure that you have the lion's share of the business available from the group you already serve. This is your *market share*.

Unless you have a stronghold in the markets you currently serve, expanding to a new market will probably be spreading your resources too thin to cover either effectively. In other words, you shouldn't consider new markets until you are very strong in the markets you already serve.

Again, a little market research will minimize the risk. How will you find new prospective customers who are likely to use the product? Since you already have a list of customers using the product, this will be a two-step process. First, establish a profile of the type of customer who buys from you now; then, find another list of prospects who match the profile (remember your sources used in Chapters 2 and 9).

The more targeted the promotion is, the more economical the process will be, and the more likely you will be to see good results.

As the chapter on direct mail (Chapter 9) emphasized, going directly to the prospects is the best way to pursue this strategy. You can compile or rent a list of qualified prospects who you have identified as likely buyers for your product.

Armed with your experience with the product and testimonials from your current satisfied customers, you will have instant credibility.

Make no mistake, this strategy takes time to work. You do not have name recognition with the new market group, so be patient. This strategy requires a larger investment than the first, in terms of both cash and time.

The highest risk of the three strategies comes with selling new products to new markets.

New products to new customers

This strategy carries the highest risk because you are selling products that you are not already familiar with, to customers who are not familiar with you. You have no track record in either of the two dimensions, customers and products.

So why would anyone pursue this risky growth strategy?

This strategy would apply if you have come up with a new product that you think has potential, but for which your current customers have no use. Or, the new product may be a variation of a current product and would simply move market share within your business.

For example, assume you are a manufacturer holding a strong market share in the high-end, new home construction industry. Your research and development department comes up with a new model design that is less expensive to buy and operate than the model that is the mainstay of your construction business.

If you promote this new product to your current customers, you will reduce your revenue from your mainstay product line. Clearly, a new customer group must be found for the new product.

Risk is high because you are spending new money in both product development and in promotion. You will also have to be patient, since it will take time to establish credibility in the new market, especially with an unproven product. This means that your return on investment will probably be slowed either by the huge promotional expense required for a quick start or by the lag in market acceptance.

Having a clear growth strategy will keep you focused on the right products, the right target customer, and your promotional strategy for the long term.

Chapter 18

Strategic Alliances

Anyone with whom you do business now, or would like to do business with in the future, is a potential marketing partner. Suppliers, customers, and other noncompeting merchants who serve the same target customer as you, all have potential as your strategic allies.

Preferred suppliers

Preferred supplier relationships are requisite for competitiveness and profitability in most industries. Depending on what business you're in, preferred supplier relationships can bring you:

> higher commission rates
>
> preferred pricing/cost of goods
>
> training
>
> financing
>
> speculative inventory
>
> promotional assistance/cooperative advertising

These benefits all looks good, but what's in it for the supplier? Why should any supplier offer you all of these goodies?

For any preferred relationship to work, it has to be an *exchange relationship*. In an exchange relationship, there is a fair exchange of value for value, and both parties are better off as a result of their participation in the relationship. In other words, an exchange relationship is a *win-win* relationship.

Notice the use of the word "both." If you are to expect special consideration from a supplier, then you must be prepared to designate a disproportionate share of your business to that supplier.

Observe the relationships national companies have with their preferred suppliers and you'll clearly see these strategies in practice. For example, you can't order a Pepsi at a McDonald's restaurant. McDonald's has a preferred supplier relationship with Coca Cola and does not even offer Pepsi. It's simply not on the menu.

Coca Cola and McDonald's work together to help make McDonald's franchises price competitive and profitable while selling more Coke. It's a *win-win* relationship. Both parties are better off as a result of their participation in the relationship.

If you do not participate in any preferred supplier relationships now, the first step is to identify to which suppliers you can direct more business while still remaining true to your target customer. The suppliers you choose will become the primary sources for your product line. Begin by consulting your preferred supplier list.

Another tactic for entering into preferred supplier relationships may be to explore the possibility of joining a consortium in your line of business. In many industries there are co-ops or consortia, groups of like businesses that use their cumulative buying power to build preferred supplier relationships. There are regional and national consortia. Often, regional groups focus on suppliers that appeal specifically to customers in their part of the country. National groups may represent more buying power, resulting in better "deals." The deals are only better, however, if the suppliers are appropriate for you and your target customer.

Look for a group that works with suppliers that you can sell with confidence, that serve your target customer well and that have brand recognition in your market.

If you prefer to stay independent, you can still have preferred supplier relationships of your own. You probably already have favorite suppliers and they're good starting points.

To help you with the process of initiating a relationship on your own, this chapter provides an outline for a preferred supplier promotion that you can use to organize your individual proposal to your target supplier.

When you approach a supplier with a formal proposal for a cooperative promotion, you demonstrate to its decision makers that you're serious about sending them business that, without you, they would not otherwise have obtained. This *incremental* business is your part of the bargain. In exchange, you are asking for promotional assistance and possibly preferential pricing (at least for the term of the promotion). By establishing this kind of relationship, you are committing yourself to perform. However, the benefit of participating in *win-win* relationships with your preferred suppliers is that they will become loyal and valuable allies.

Proposal Outline
Preferred Supplier Promotion

I. Purpose
A. State the objectives of the promotion
1. Consumer Awareness
2. Promote a specific Product
B. Projected sales resulting from promotion
1. Quote figures from similar past promotions
II. Media
A. State specifically how you plan to reach consumers
1. Print Media
a. Number and frequency of ads over duration of the promotion
b. Mock-up of proposed ad layout and copy
2. Direct mail program
a. Number of pieces to be mailed
b. Source and qualification of mail list
(1.) Internal Customer & Prospect lists
(2.) Demographics/Buying History of names
c. Mock-up of proposed mailer layout and copy
3. Stuffers, Flyers, Posters, etc.
a. Distribution and display
b. Mock-up of proposed promotional pieces
4. Other media
5. Office Display
B. Examples from past promotions.
1. Copies of Print ads, Mailers, etc.
C. Support Materials from Supplier
1. Brochures, Shells, Postcards, Point of Sale Displays, etc.
III. Staff Awareness
A. Training
1. Request sales training session from Sales Rep.
2. Request product samples
IV. Cost Breakdown
A. Complete breakdown of cost of promotion.
1. Media Advertising (X insertions @ $0.00)
2. Mail Cost (X pieces @ $0.00)
3. Printing Expense (All relevant printing costs)
4. Display Cost
B. Proposed Co-op funding (As % of total cost of promotion)
V. Sales Incentives
A. Staff sales incentives during promotion
1. Our own cash incentives
2. Supplier incentives
B. Override incentives for sales thresholds

Customers

Similar relationships can be developed with your customers. You know that referrals, or word-of-mouth advertising, constitute the strongest form of advertising. There is no better recommendation than one that comes from a satisfied customer. Customers who are referred to you this way are "presold" when they come to you.

So, how do you go about enlisting your existing customers as good-will ambassadors? Well, you have to ask them! This may sound oversimplified, but it really is true. They may tell their friends about the great product they bought, but you want to make sure they also tell them where they bought it.

Building referral business takes patience. You have to first establish a relationship with the existing customer. If you follow up after each sale, you will soon find the customers who are delighted with you. Concentrate on your repeat customers. They're clearly sold on you and are candidates for ambassadorships. First-time buyers, no matter how satisfied, have to know you better before they rave to their friends about you.

It's been said that most people have a "sphere of influence" of some 250 people, including friends, family, business associates, and fellow association or club members. It's likely that each of your happy customers knows more than one person who is a likely prospect for you.

The question, "Do you know someone who could use our service?" is too general. Narrow the field of possibilities by specifying the type of person you serve. For instance, if you specialize in fine cookware, you might ask your customers about their friends who also enjoy entertaining.

Rewarding referrals

Any time a customer refers new business to you, you should do something to reward him or her.

It doesn't have to be expensive. In fact, in many cases, customers may be embarrassed by receiving a gift. A simple thank you note or telephone call may be sufficient. (When a happy customer refers a new speaking engagement to me, I always send flowers or a small business-related gift in appreciation.)

You may set up a formal reward program, offering discounts, coupons, or even cash rewards for referrals. One credit card offers bonus frequent flyer miles for every new customer referred.

Depending on the nature of your business, rewarding referrals may be formal or informal. In either case, do it! There is no better business than a "presold" referral and no one can sell your products better than an unbiased, happy customer.

Chapter 19

Five Indispensable Marketing Tools for the New Millennium

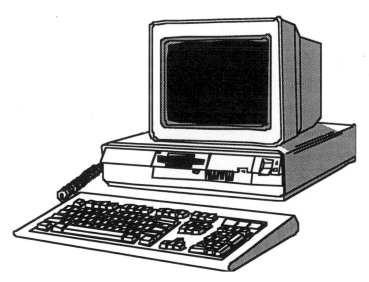

As a small business owner, you compete with the Goliaths of the business world every day—the chain stores, the ware house stores, the national and international corporations. Fortunately for you, people still prefer to go where they are made to feel welcome, comfortable and appreciated.

These natural tendencies offer opportunities that the small business owner must use to his or her advantage. In this light, here are presented *five indispensable marketing tools for the new millennium.*

1. Data based marketing

As we move from an age of mass production and mass communication, to an age of customization and individualization, sophisticated consumers of the 1990s and beyond will patronize the businesses that respond to their needs and desires, not the ones that expect them to adapt to a product or service that has a one-size-fits-all design.

Therefore, to be successful in the coming age, you will have to know everything you can about your customers so you can anticipate their needs and desires, and design products and services just for them.

To differentiate yourself from your competitors, you must learn things about your customer that your competitor doesn't know. This demands a very personal relationship with each of your customers. Your relationship with your customers resembles a courtship; you will have to work hard to establish the relationship and even harder to maintain it. You'll have to come up with ways of pleasing them as no other business can, and you can never let up. You will find that customers become more demanding as the relationship continues and that they expect you to remember every important thing they say to you.

It's an information age. You most important function is obtaining, storing, and processing information about your customers, and using that information to establish and maintain unique relationships with each one. You must anticipate their needs and fill them before they start looking for the solutions. Remind me of Dad's birthday before I've started thinking about what to get him and you win the first shot at my business!

2. Interactive technology

The Information Highway is coming to your town and it will impact every retail business in the coming years.

You can stand idly by as the Goliaths devour your market share, or you can act now to compete in the electronic marketplace. Interactive technology doesn't necessarily mean having a web sight on the internet. In the coming years, it will take either a tremendous amount of money to place yourself where internet surfers will see you, or a product so unique that it will stand out in the crowd.

Many businesses will try the information superhighway and end up as roadkill in a year or two.

In coming years, we will all have access to interactive television. Home Shopping Network was a pioneer, offering a video catalogue throughout the day and night. In the very near future, each of us will have a box connected to our television, through which we will be able to go directly to the product we're looking for at any time, select from several suppliers, and order without getting up out of the recliner.

The consumer of the 1990s and beyond is totally comfortable with this kind of technology. Even those who do not choose to "surf the internet" through a home or business computer will be able to embrace interactive TV.

3. Fax-on-demand

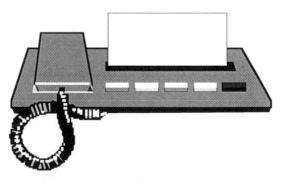

With fax-on-demand, you can offer your product information instantly and automatically, day and night. This capability is available from service providers who scan your information into their computer, and assign a code to each item that may be requested. The callers simply enter the code and their fax numbers, and the requested information is faxed to them.

Fax-on-demand is used as a response medium for broadcast advertising. If you are going to use broadcast advertising, it's important that you have a response medium that is easy, free of charge to the prospect and fast. Nothing gets a piece of paper in their hands faster than fax-on-demand.

It's available now and it's surprisingly inexpensive.

4. Articles

One of the best ways to demonstrate your expertise is to submit articles to trade magazines. If you have a talent for writing, you have access to thousands of people whom you would otherwise spend a fortune to reach by advertising.

If you serve a specific industry, find all the magazines you can that are published for its members. To begin, write a letter to the magazine's editor suggesting your topic, with a brief synopsis of the proposed article.

When you submit your article, be aware that it will be edited to fit the space allocated and to remove any characteristics of and "infomercial."

By writing articles, your intention should be to share your expertise and nothing more. Your name will appear in the byline and readers are usually provided with information on how to contact you at the end of the article.

Submit articles regularly so you achieve some visibility through repetition. You won't see much in the line of direct response from your articles, but you will develop a profile in your field. When people see one of your advertisements or mail pieces, they'll be more likely to recognize the name.

You can also use reprints of your articles in recognized magazines as enclosures in your direct mail or as excerpts in your newsletter. Having been published in national trade magazines underscores your credibility in your local market.

5. Seminars

Providing training in your area of expertise is a great way to develop rapport with people. In this age of information, those who have it and are willing to share it will have a tremendous advantage. If yours is a business that can provide information that will improve people's lives, finances, families, or careers, you can reach people by offering seminars.

As with articles, bear in mind that you are sharing information, not producing infomercials. Certainly people realize that one of your motives is to build your business. But if you do so by establishing yourself as an expert, if the information you have to share is truly valuable and you present it professionally, you will establish a trust factor that will make you a first choice if they need the kinds of services you provide.

By leading seminars, you will be meeting prospective customers and it's important to maintain those new contacts. Add them to your mailing list for a limited time, send them your newsletter for six months—do something to follow up.

Presenting educational seminars is a great way to meet new prospects, add qualified names to your mailing list and all at no expense to you!

You may present seminars in your own office if you have the space or you may rent a hotel meeting room. Some attendees, with the hope of avoiding a heavy sales pitch, are likely to prefer the neutrality of a hotel meeting room. You may be able to present seminars at a local community college or adult education program. If you truly are an expert in your field, and you have information that people can use, get in front of the room and make it known!

Suggested reading

Canfield, Jack and Mark Victor Hansen. *Chicken Soup for the Soul*. Dearfield Beach, FL: Health Communications, Inc. ,1993. "101 Stories to Open the Heart and Rekindle the Spirit."

Carnie, Dale. *The Quick and Easy Way to Effective Speaking*. Garden City, NY: Dorothy Carnegie, 1962. (Revision by Dorothy Carnegie, author of *Public Speaking and Influencing Men in Business*)

Gnam, Rene. *Direct Mail Workshop*. Englewood Cliffs, NJ: Prentice-Hall, 1989. "1,001 ideas, tips, rule breakers & brainstorms for improving profits fast."

Holz, Herman. *Great Promo Pieces*. New York: John Wiley & Sons, Ltd., 1988. "Create your own Brochures, Broadsides, Ads, Flyers, and Newsletters that Get Results."

Mersereau, Larry, CTC. *Direct Mail Strategies for Independent Sales Agents*. Des Moines, IA: Larry

Mersereau Assoc., 1994. "Your guide to effective and economical direct mail promotion."

Roane, Susan. *How to Work a Room*. New York: Warner Books, 1989. "Learn the strategies of savvy socializing for business and personal success."

Look for all these and other fine Griffin Books
at your favorite bookstore or write to:

GRIFFIN PUBLISHING

Date _____

ne _____

npany _____

ress _____

State _____ Zip _____

ne ( ) _____ - _____

	PRICE	QTY.	AMOUNT
estring Marketing L. Mersereau	$14.95		
repreneurial Transitions R. Cammarano Provides the tools and solutions needed to create effective organizational structure for your business.	$16.95		
r Money & Your Home Sidney Lenz A step-by-step guide to financing or refinancing your home.	$12.95		
Ison on Change Terry Paulson, Ph.D. A compilation of quotes, commentary and questions to stimulate thought and discussion.	$12.95		
born on Success Mark Sanborn Practical ideas on how to achieve more of what you want in life.	$12.95		
Sub-total			
CA res. add 8.25%			
Shipping			
TOTAL			

ping:
First book $2.50
Add'l. books $1.00 each

ck type of payment:

___ Check or money order enclosed

___ VISA   _____ Mastercard

t.# _____

Date _____

ature _____

Send order to:
Griffin Publishing
544 W. Colorado St.
Glendale, CA 91204
Or call to order:
1-800-423-5789